Atlanta at Table

Atlanta at Table

By Frances Schultz

Photographs by Dot Griffith

Foreword by Ryan Gainey

WYRICK & COMPANY

To Mama, my best editor and my best friend

A Tarboro Book

Published by Wyrick & Company
Post Office Box 89
Charleston, South Carolina 29402

Copyright © 1996 by Frances Schultz
All rights reserved

Set in Sabon with Gill Sans and Kuenstler Script display
by Books International, Norcross, Georgia
Printed and bound in Hong Kong
Designed by Sandra Strother Hudson

Library of Congress Cataloging-in-Publication Data

Schultz, Frances, 1957–
Atlanta at table / by Frances Schultz : photographs by Dot
Griffith : foreword by Ryan Gainey.
p. cm.
"A Tarboro book"--T.p. verso.
Includes index.
ISBN 0-941711-33-1 (alk. paper)
1. Cookery, American--Southern style.   2. Cookery--Georgia--
Atlanta.   3. Menus.   4. Entertaining--Georgia--Atlanta.   5. Atlanta
(Ga.)--Social life and customs. I. Title.
TX715.2.S68S38   1996
641.5975—dc20   96-14019

All photographs in this book were taken by Dot Griffith,
except the following: Thomas Birdwell, back jacket and pages
100, 103, 104, 107, 124, 128, 131, 148, 153, 154; Terry
Eilers, 142, Richard Hughes, 64, 70; James Landon, back jacket
flap; Bob Libby, 40 (courtesy of Atlanta Steeplechase);
Frances Schultz, 68.

Contents

Foreword

*L*ike most Southerners, I learned my best manners from sitting at the table. Directions to sit up straight, say the blessing, and not interrupt were as much a part of the meal as the meat and potatoes. That was the kitchen table where I grew up, in Hartsville, South Carolina. We were not wealthy. My mother's table was simple but satisfying. And yet the experience was rich. Because "at table" is not only where I began to learn manners; it is where I began to learn life. And looking back, I see it as all being bound together.

Those early days at the table have developed into a passion for very good food and an insatiable appetite for creative table accessories—the cloths, the napkins, the plates, the silver (or whatever), the stemware. And my years of gardening with vegetables, herbs and flowers, and bringing their bounty to the table have enriched the creative aspects not just of table settings but of everyday life. Sometimes it is about entertaining; sometimes about simply sustaining.

That is as true in small towns, Southern and otherwise, as it is in big cities, like Atlanta, where I have spent the majority of my adult years. And I have delighted in observing its changes. About twenty-five years ago there was a quiet, unnoticed influx of creative spirit that migrated into Atlanta and became a part of the dream that is embodied in the symbol of this city—the phoenix—burgeoning, rising up from the ashes. This group of people quickly began to participate in the cultural and business life of Atlanta, contributing to the hastening pace that flows through the inner circles of our city life.

Atlanta vibrates with this kind of integration, and it continues with the city's increasing ethnic diversity, blending with the grace and charm that make Atlanta still a small Southern town. Cultural and social events once limited to an elite group are now a part of everyday life, as all of us bring our own unique and personal expression to the table—whether it's good old barbecue take-out, a picnic in the park while the Atlanta Symphony performs, or a candlelit dinner at Chastain, where everyone goes to a lot of trouble to set the finest table, to be seen and to be eating the best.

Things are not what they used to be; they're better, as is our appreciation, perhaps, for sharing the most satiable aspects of life: food and fellowship.

Atlanta today has more restaurants with as varied styles and geographic influences as there are herbs and spices. Caterers for all occasions fill the yellow pages. Quality food-to-go is a mainstay—and I don't mean hamburgers and french fries.

So where is the table in all this activity? Well, for me it's still in the kitchen—at least the soul of it abides there. But that table is a creative palette in and of itself, and where you set it doesn't matter—on the ground, in the garden, on your lap or at a charity ball. How you set it, what you eat, and with whom make the difference. You are free to imagine the options, and to enjoy exploring them. Atlanta offers so many these days.

We are partaking in the spice of life. Therefore, make every meal memorable, and celebrate every birthday, anniversary, holiday or any occasion with gusto and glee. For to do so is to celebrate the true sustenance of life—the pleasures of a table well set, well served, and shared.

RYAN GAINEY

Acknowledgements

Writing can be a lonely business, so it is especially nice to look back on it and realize that one was never really alone. I am grateful once again to my editor and publisher Pete Wyrick for his steadfastness and good sense, and for his confidence in me and my work; and to Connie Wyrick, Anne Hanahan, Michael Robertson and Kay Wise for seeing to so many details.

Ryan Gainey has not only written a lovely foreword, he has helped shape the heart and soul of this book, and without him it would not be complete—in truth it wouldn't even be legitimate, for Ryan's vision and spirit have so infused entertaining in Atlanta that no book on that subject would be complete without him.

Next would have to come my mother, Ruth Clark, and my assistant Aimee Chubb, without whose intelligence, advice, encouragement, cooking, criticism and support I honestly don't think I could have worked through this project as successfully as (I hope) I have. And I know I couldn't have done it without my small army of advisors and cooks whose opinions and expertise were invaluable: Alisa Barry of Bella Cucina, Laurie Bray, Mary Bray, Smith Hanes, Alex Hitz, Jim Landon, Elizabeth Long, Elizabeth James of The Company Co., Jenny Johnston, Angie Bennett Mosier, Candy Sheehan and Caroline Trask. And a special nod to Duvall Fuqua, who, upon testing one of the dishes recounted to me, as only a sister could, that she and her husband Rex took one bite, looked at each other, and burst out laughing. (I left that one out, in case you were wondering.)

Thanks to principal photographer Dot Griffith and to photographers Thomas Birdwell, Terry Eilers, Richard Hughes, and Bob Libby, for their work which fills these pages with color and life; and to Sandra Strother Hudson for her beautiful and thoughtful book design. And, in addition to those already mentioned, to Boo Beasley, Sadie Brooks, Dolores Hall, Rena Harris, David MacGilvray, Anne Louise Rutherford, and Kathy Servick for their treasured recipes.

If I could write a hug, I'd write one for all my friends and family for always being there, including Howell Morrison, Haloli Richter and Henry Ross, and for the folks of Atlanta whose hospitality and style inspired this book, and whose generous invitations made it possible.

Introduction

With my first book, *Atlanta at Home*, I wanted to tell stories about Atlanta through people and their places. With this, *Atlanta at Table*, the stories of Atlanta are through people and their parties—with a very loose interpretation of the word "party." In varied settings in and about Atlanta, this book is for gatherings of friends and family at table, or some semblance of a table, be it a blanket under a tree, around the kitchen table at home, dressed up in the dining room, or decked out at a fancy ball. As I've lived and worked in Atlanta, and as this life and work have taken me all over the world, I've come to understand that inherent in our experience at table is also an experience of place. We have our place at the table, yes, but the table itself has a place in something, too—in culture, in society, in time, in our lives. Here is an insight into the energy, creativity, and, to some degree, the culinary tendencies of folks in Atlanta, as well as a firsthand look at our fabled Southern hospitality, which is alive and well—and well fed.

Which brings me to the subjects of food and cooking. I didn't really expect to write a cookbook, but once I realized that was where this project was headed, I set for myself a standard that was both high and humble. I, maybe like you, have a handful of cookbooks I am devoted to because I trust them; I know whatever I make from them will either be good or great. I want this book to be one of those. Not huge, not fancy, not even all that innovative. Just good. OK, real good. I also wanted the recipes to be easy enough for the novice cook and healthy enough for any conscience. I've tried to eliminate fat grams where they were gratuitous and include them where they are worth it, like in desserts.

As to the idea of entertaining in general, if I can impart any message it is to relax and just do it. I've tried to plan the menus and recipes according to how I think most people really can or do entertain, not according to how they *wished* or think they *should* entertain. You do not have to be Superwoman or Martha Stewart to have a memorable meal or party. I mean, how many times have you been ungrateful for another's hospitality because he or she had not hand-painted gold leaf borders around the starched linen napkins or hadn't frozen rosebuds into all the ice cubes?

That's what I thought. It's time and trouble enough to entertain (and I love doing it), but I'm not into making candied violets or weaving leek greens into wreaths around mashed potatoes, and I'm just not going to worry about it. I figure people are glad to be invited and just as glad not to be doing it themselves.

And finally, whether your home is in Atlanta, or somewhere far away, I hope this book and the spirit in which it is written will give you a unique window on our city, and will inspire and enrich your sharing at table—whatever you're serving, wherever you are.

Blessings.

Atlanta at Table

The Swan House Ball

*S*wan House, on the grounds of the Atlanta History Center, is the site of the annual Swan House Ball, begun in 1986. And because of its elegant surroundings—the 1928 classical house and gardens designed by Philip Shutze—the Ball has become a nonpareil, over the years raising hundreds of thousands of dollars for the Atlanta Historical Society.

Under a grand white tent at the base of a double stair and cascading fountain, designer Dennis Schuhart created "American Splendor." Inspired by the era during which *Swan House* was built, the American splendor of the 1920s saw a revival of classical style adroitly executed by the legendary American decorator Elsie de Wolfe and her contemporaries. Of her several prominent protégées-in-spirit was Ruby Ross Wood, a native of Monticello, Georgia, and the original decorator for *Swan House*.

For the ball, as Elsie herself might have ordered, the tables were draped in a beige shadow stripe, and chair cushions were covered in leopard. Elaborate mirrored lamps by David Little were centerpieces as would befit the chicest nightclubs, and the tent poles were transformed into Egyptian-esque fluted columns. There was a nightclub-style bar—a different touch for a charity ball—and a black and white dance floor. Floral impresario Michal Evans placed white orchids and ivy around the lamps, filled silver wine coolers with peonies, and arranged Casablanca lilies in tall, slender vases trailing ivy and elaeagnus. Tiffany & Co. treated the ladies to a pair of crystal candlesticks, and Neiman-Marcus gave perfumes.

Guests danced to and marveled at the all-female Kit McClure Band, followed with pop tunes spun by Chris Miller. The 1992 ball was chaired by Carol Rohrig; honorary chairmen were Mr. and Mrs. J. Mack Robinson. Dinner included salmon with lime and fennel, grilled tenderloin and roast quail. Accompaniments were a squash and zucchini timbale, sweet potato coins, and salad of summer field greens. Dessert was a fresh blackberry dacquoise layered with meringue, nuts and berries.

Our menu is no less elegant, but quite a bit less complicated.

Menu

Poached Leeks in Lemon Curry Vinaigrette

Roast Veal With Mustard Sauce and Orzo Primavera

Caramel and Hazelnut Pôts de Crème

SERVES 8

This menu is as delicious—sumptuous, I daresay—as it is impressive. Leeks are an oft-served first course in French bistros, but a bit unusual here in the States . . . maybe you'll start something. Steamed whole artichokes with lemon butter would be a wonderful starter as well. The orzo can be done a day (or even two days) ahead. The veal does need babysitting in terms of basting, but once out of the oven, it can sit a while, covered, and won't suffer a smidgen. The pôts de crème can be made up to three days in advance—the elegantly perfect dinner party dessert.

Poached Leeks in Lemon Curry Vinaigrette

An unusual and pretty first course, with a European flair. Allow 1 to 2 leeks per person. If they are nice and fat (the leeks, that is), 1 per person should be enough.

Poached Leeks

8 to 16 leeks, depending on size   2 large tomatoes, chopped

Leeks are sandy. To prepare them for cooking, leave the root end intact and trim the top 2 or 3 inches of the green part. Remove any blemished or tough outer leaves, and cut the leeks in half lengthwise, stopping about an inch short of the root end. Soak in cold water or rinse well under running water, separating the leaves and rinsing the sand from between them.

Bring a large pot of salted water to boil and add the leeks. Reduce heat and simmer for 7 to 10 minutes, until white part is tender when pierced with a knife. Remove and refrigerate until ready to use.

To serve, slice leeks into slivers lengthwise and garnish with a dollop of chopped tomato across them. Pour dressing over.

Lemon Curry Vinaigrette

2 tablespoons lemon juice

1 tablespoon sherry vinegar

2 tablespoons Dijon mustard

1 teaspoon mayonnaise

1 teaspoon curry powder

1 large garlic clove, crushed

4 anchovy filets, drained (optional)

1/4 teaspoon freshly ground black pepper

1/4 teaspoon salt (may omit if including anchovies)

3/4 cup extra virgin olive oil

In food processor or blender combine all ingredients except oil. (You may also do this in a bowl with a whisk, but finely mince the anchovies first.) Add the oil in a thin, steady stream, until dressing is smooth and creamy.

Roast Veal With Mustard Sauce and Orzo Primavera

A heavenly dish. The veal is a bit costly, but worth it! As to the cut, a loin roast is spectacular but costs about a million dollars. I've found that the less expensive shoulder roast works beautifully. Ask your butcher to trim, bone and roll it for you. Veal cooks more quickly than beef, so you won't be at it all day.

Roast Veal With Mustard Sauce

3 to 4 pound veal roast, trimmed, boned and rolled

6 tablespoons butter, softened

3/4 cup Dijon mustard

1/4 cup sherry

1 (10 1/2-ounce) can beef consommé, undiluted

1 tablespoon cornstarch, if desired

1/4 cup fresh chopped parsley

Heat oven to 325°. Combine softened butter and mustard and pour over meat in Dutch oven, covering completely. Cover and roast about 20 to 25 minutes per pound, so 1 to 1½ hours, total. While veal is roasting, warm sherry and consommé together in a saucepan and use it to baste veal every 15 minutes. Use it all. Remove veal from oven and let rest 20 to 30 minutes before slicing.

Meanwhile, for the sauce, you may either serve the pan juices, strained, as they are, or make a thicker type gravy using the cornstarch as follows: Pour about 2½ cups of the juices into a saucepan. Take 2 tablespoons out and put into a small, separate bowl. Add the cornstarch and combine to make a smooth paste. Return mixture to the saucepan and stir over medium-low heat. Serve sauce separately, sprinkled with parsley. This sauce is always a huge hit.

Orzo Primavera

This is delicious and very pretty on the plate. Orzo, when cooked, resembles large grains of rice—sort of like risotto but without the last-minute trouble. I like using asparagus in spring and broccoli in fall, but the availability of both year-round always leaves you the option.

1 tablespoon salt	¼ cup plus ¼ cup grated
1 cup asparagus tips or	Parmesan cheese
small broccoli florets	Grated zest of 1 lemon
1 cup shredded, thinly sliced	(about 1 teaspoon)
or julienned carrots	2 tablespoons butter
1 cup grated, thinly sliced	2 tablespoons olive oil
or julienned zucchini	2 tablespoons thinly sliced onion
½ cup finely chopped	2 cloves garlic, minced
red or yellow bell pepper	1 cup chicken stock
1 cup frozen green peas, thawed	1 cup white wine
½ cup chopped fresh basil	1 pound orzo pasta

Have a large empty pot in the sink and bring another large pot of water to a rolling boil, add 1 tablespoon of salt, and blanch asparagus or broccoli, carrots, zucchini and peppers for 1 minute. Add peas at the last second, then drain all in a colander over the pot in the sink, and use this same water later for cooking your pasta.

The Swan House Ball, held every spring to benefit the Atlanta History Center, is considered one of the season's most elegant events. Designer Dennis Schuhart created the swank, 1930s nightclub look for the party, complemented by floral designer Michal Evans's sumptuous all-white arrangements.

Mix basil, Parmesan and lemon peel, and reserve.

In a medium saucepan, melt 2 tablespoons butter with 2 tablespoons olive oil. Add 2 tablespoons thinly sliced onion and 2 cloves minced garlic, and sauté until soft. Add 1 cup each of chicken stock and white wine, and bring to a boil. Reduce heat and simmer, stirring, about 5 minutes, or until liquid is reduced by about one fourth. Add basil mixture, then add all into vegetables and stir to combine. Dish may be prepared up to this point and covered and set aside or refrigerated overnight.

Make pasta according to package directions. Drain, but do not run water over it—the starch still on the pasta helps the sauce adhere to it. Add pasta to vegetables, toss, and serve with a little extra Parmesan sprinkled on top—but don't overdo; it will compete with your veal sauce.

If you want to make the entire dish ahead, sprinkle with the remaining Parmesan cheese, cover, and refrigerate. When ready to serve, bring to room temperature, uncover and warm for 15 minutes at 350° before serving. It does not need to be piping hot.

Caramel and Hazelnut Pôts de Crème

Creamy and rich, yet not too heavy, this traditional favorite has a little surprise in store. It is really a simple baked custard, but with to-die-for caramel sauce on the bottom and a light hazelnut crust on top, formed as the nuts and the butter from the caramel rise to the surface during baking. I wish I could say this was the result of a master chef working her wonders, but it was a blind pig (me) finding an acorn. And if I do say so myself, an acorn never tasted so good. You need a candy thermometer for the sauce. Don't let the long recipe deter you. It is easy and goof-proof.

Caramel Sauce

2/3 cup chopped toasted
   hazelnuts (or pecans)
4 tablespoons (1/2 stick) butter
1/2 cup packed brown sugar

1/4 cup cream
1 tablespoon hazelnut liqueur, such as
   Frangelico (optional)
1/8 teaspoon salt

Heat oven to 350°. Spread nuts on a cookie sheet and toast for 5 to 10 minutes until fragrant and lightly browned. If you like, rub the skins from the hazelnuts before chopping. Chop the nuts into small pieces but not crumbs—do so by hand and not food processor. In a small saucepan over medium heat, melt the butter and sugar together and stir in the cream. Bring to a boil, then reduce heat again and cook until it reaches the soft ball stage on the candy thermometer, 230°. Remove from heat and stir in liqueur (if using) and salt. Evenly divide the mixture among 8 ramekins. Sprinkle each with a layer of chopped nuts, and set aside.

Pôts de Crème

1 ¼ cups heavy cream	3 eggs
1 cup milk	2 egg yolks
2 teaspoons vanilla	⅓ cup plus 2 tablespoons sugar
2 tablespoons hazelnut liqueur, such as Frangelico	

In heavy saucepan over medium heat, bring combined cream and milk to a boil, reduce heat slightly and cook about 1 minute. Stir in vanilla and liqueur and remove from heat. In a separate bowl, preferably one you can easily pour with, whisk together eggs, yolks and sugar.

Adding the hot milk to the eggs can cook the eggs, so it must be done gradually: Whisk about ¼ cup of the hot milk mixture into the egg mixture and then gradually add the rest. Don't worry about the skin that forms on the milk; it dissolves by itself. If it bothers you, though, strain the mixture into another bowl or pitcher before proceeding.

Heat the oven to 300°. Place the 8 caramel-nut-lined ramekins in a large roasting pan. Pour the custard mixture into the ramekins and place in oven. Pour water in the pan to reach halfway up the sides of the ramekins and bake 25 to 30 minutes, until custard is set but still a little shaky in the middle. It continues to cook after you take it out. Remove ramekins from water and cool on a rack, then refrigerate. Serve chilled or at room temperature.

Variations

Add 2 ounces of semisweet chocolate to the cream-milk mixture so it melts as the mixture boils and adds a subtle chocolate essence to the custard. You may also add 1 teaspoon of coffee or espresso powder, alone or with the chocolate, for a coffee or mocha flavor. Any of the three are complemented by the caramel and nuts.

Al Fresco Elegance

*A*tlanta is known for its lush, leafy suburbs built among rolling hills and wide avenues. It has even been accused, in a back-handed compliment, of being "a forest looking for a city." The northwest Atlanta areas of Buckhead and Sandy Springs come to mind; as do Ansley Park and Sherwood Forest in Midtown; Druid Hills, Morningside and Virginia Highlands in the northeast; Inman Park with its grand old Victorian houses in the southeast; and Cascade Heights and West End in the southwest.

The city, and of course much of the South in general, is also known for its lovely, soft-colored springs and its crisp, richly hued autumns. In fact (let's not talk about July and August), there are fairly long periods of mildness which make for ample opportunity to entertain outdoors. In the fall, all Atlanta's trees turn for one last, brilliant show before their winter snooze. Awakening in the spring, gardens brim with hydrangeas and roses, and roadsides are abloom in dogwood and wisteria. Indeed, much of the decorating is done for you. All you have to do is provide the setting and the supper.

The occasion may take many forms, from an old quilt spread on the grass in Piedmont Park or on the banks of the Chattahoochee, to a table and chairs set up in the garden, to an elegant seated dinner like the one pictured here at the home of Suzanne and Ed Inman. Making full use of their city's mild climate and indulging the typical Southerner's love for the garden, the Inmans had the foresight to request a space in their house for outdoor entertaining, and the late post-modernist architect Charles Moore had the vision to create it.

Now, the meal. Of utmost importance is doing it ahead. If you can set up a sort of buffet, and cover everything until serving time, do so. If something needs to be chilled, set it on a bed of ice or in a cooler camouflaged by a tablecloth or pretty sarong wrapped around it. Set up the bar nearby as well. The less running back and forth to the house, the better—unless you have energetic help. You will want to be outside with your guests, not inside with your stove. It will make all the difference in your enjoyment of the evening, and most importantly, of one another.

ENU

Chilled Shrimp and Cucumber Soup

**Grilled Beef Tenderloin Salad With Roasted Red Peppers,
Vidalia Onions and Snow Peas**

Buttery Pull-Apart Bread

Toffee-Oatmeal-Cookie "Napoleons"

SERVES 12

This is easily halved to serve six. Elizabeth James's recipe for Grilled Beef Tender-loin Salad calls for a sour cream dressing, but I've substituted a vinaigrette for this menu since it includes a yogurt-based soup and frozen yogurt dessert, and therefore more than enough dairy. I include Elizabeth's sour cream dressing, however, and it is wonderful. If you like, make it anyway and serve it on the side. Or try it with, say, an asparagus or green beans vinaigrette first course and a simple fresh fruit tart for dessert.

Chilled Shrimp and Cucumber Soup

This is always a hit, refreshing and yet substantial. I use canned tomato soup or bisque, and if that bothers you, trust me. It seasons the soup just-right, and after one taste, you'll at least take an exception to your canned soup snob attitude. I'm grateful for the recipe from family friend Dolores Hall, who guards her many culinary treasures closely.

4 medium cucumbers, peeled,
   seeded and diced, sprinkled with salt,
   then rinsed and patted dry
   after 30 minutes
¾ pound of shrimp, cooked
   and chopped

2 cups tomato soup or tomato bisque
2 cups chicken stock
6 cups plain yogurt (nonfat OK)
2 cups cream (skim milk OK)
4 garlic cloves, crushed
Fresh chopped parsley for garnish

Combine all ingredients and refrigerate. Sprinkle with parsley before serving.

Grilled Beef Tenderloin Salad With Roasted Red Peppers, Vidalia Onions and Snow Peas

This makes a beautiful presentation and is very satisfying. Make it several hours in advance so the vegetables have a chance to marinate.

4 pounds beef tenderloin
6 red peppers, roasted and
   cut in strips
¾ pound snow peas (may
   substitute sugar snap peas)

1 large Vidalia onion (or red onion), very
   thinly sliced
1 or 2 heads Bibb or Romaine lettuce

Roast (or grill) the tenderloin until rare—internal temperature should be about 130°. If roasting, begin with the oven temperature at 425°. After 15 minutes reduce heat to 350°. As a rule, allow 10 to 12 minutes per pound. When cool, slice thinly and cut into bite-size pieces.

To roast red peppers, adjust oven rack to top position and turn on broiler. Lightly brush pan with olive oil. Cut peppers in half and remove stem and seeds. Place on pan skin side up and broil 3 to 4 minutes until skin is charred and blistered. Place peppers in a paper bag and close the top. This steams the peppers, and the skins will slide off easily after 5 minutes or so. Slice in ¾-inch wide strips.

Prepare dressing using recipe below.

Bring large pot of water to boil and blanch peas for 30 seconds. Drain.

Combine all ingredients except beef and lettuce with ½ cup of dressing, and let marinate in the refrigerator for 2 hours or longer. Add beef and serve on lettuce leaves with remaining dressing on the side.

Dijon Vinaigrette With Fresh Herbs

Without the herbs, this is a wonderful, basic dressing. For this salad, however, the basil and thyme are good flavors for the beef and the peppers. If you do not have fresh herbs, substitute a teaspoon each of the dried.

$^1/_4$ cup wine vinegar (red or white)
1 tablespoon Dijon mustard
2 cloves garlic, minced
1 tablespoon fresh basil, chopped

1 tablespoon fresh thyme, chopped
$^2/_3$ cup olive oil
Salt and freshly ground pepper

Combine first five ingredients and whisk in olive oil in a slow, thin stream. Season to taste.

Variations

To the above dressing add either or both of the following: 4 ounces crumbled goat cheese and 1 or 2 tablespoons of finely chopped sundried tomatoes*

*If tomatoes are dried, measure $^1/_3$ cup tomatoes into small bowl and pour 1 cup boiling water over them. Soak for 15 minutes, drain, and finely chop. If the tomatoes are the oil-packed kind, use as they are. Just drain and finely chop.

Sour Cream Dressing

You could also make this with yogurt.

2 cups sour cream (or yogurt)

1/3 cup grainy mustard

2 tablespoons fresh lemon juice

3 garlic cloves, minced

Salt and freshly ground pepper

Combine all ingredients and season to taste.

Buttery Pull-Apart Bread

This is an altered version of a sublime Southern creation called "Monkey Bread," a recipe for which appears in almost every Southern Junior League cookbook since The Flood. I've adapted this from several of those and bake it in two loaf pans instead of the conventional one tube pan, but you may do either. Moist, dense and with a touch of sweetness, it couldn't be anything but homemade. And while it calls for pulling apart rather than cutting, I confess I've sliced it a day or two old for tomato sandwiches. And oh boy, they were something.

1/2 cup sugar

1 1/2 teaspoons salt

1 cup mashed potatoes
   (about 1 large potato)

1 package dry yeast

1/2 cup warm water

1 cup (2 sticks) plus 4 tablespoons
   (1/2 stick) butter

1 cup milk

5 3/4 cups sifted flour

2 eggs

Combine sugar, salt and potatoes in large bowl. In a small, separate bowl, dissolve yeast in warm water. Melt 1 cup butter over low heat and stir in milk, then add to potato mixture. Add yeast and 3 cups of flour. Beat eggs with remaining flour and add to the other mixture.

Cover with a kitchen towel and let rise at room temperature for 1 hour. Then punch it down, cover again, and refrigerate until ready to bake, up to a day in advance.

When ready to bake, grease two loaf pans and heat oven to 350°. Melt remaining butter in a bowl and set aside. Punch the dough down again and form into balls about 1 1/2 inches in diameter. Dip each piece of dough in butter and place in loaf pan, making two layers of balls. Bake 30 to 40 minutes, until golden brown on top.

To serve, pull bread apart (or pass and let guests do it) instead of cutting it. To re-warm it, wrap with foil and warm in oven. It also freezes well.

Toffee-Oatmeal-Cookie "Napoleons"

These are not only yummy, but different and fun! What they are, really, are good ol' ice cream sandwiches, and everyone loves them. The recipe comes from my assist-ant, Aimee Chubb. You may experiment with different kinds of ice cream—toffee, praline, chocolate, mocha! And I've devised two variations for dressing them up a bit, if it's a special occasion.

1 cup all-purpose flour

½ teaspoon baking soda

¼ teaspoon salt

¼ teaspoon cinnamon

1 stick of butter, softened

½ cup sugar

½ cup dark brown sugar, tightly packed

1 egg

1 teaspoon vanilla

1 cup old fashioned rolled oats

½ cup chopped chocolate-toffee candy (about 2 [1.4-ounce] candy bars, such as Heath or Skor bars)

1 quart vanilla (or other flavor) frozen yogurt or ice cream, softened at room temperature before using

Grease or non-stick spray cookie sheet (or two cookie sheets, if you have them), and heat oven to 350°. Sift together flour, soda, salt and cinnamon. In large bowl, cream butter and sugars. Mix in egg and vanilla. Add flour mixture, oats and chopped candy. This will make 24 cookies of uniform size. Place six balls per cookie sheet (they spread a lot), then moisten fingers and flatten each ball into a 2 ¾-inch round. Bake 13 to 15 minutes, until golden. The cookies are brittle, so handle with care.

To make sandwiches, spread scant ⅓ cup frozen yogurt over bottom of 1 cookie. Top with another cookie. The topsides of each cookie should be facing out. Wrap in plastic wrap and freeze. Store flat; otherwise the soft ice cream will ooze out at the bottom.

"Dressed Up" Variation I

These are so pretty and so festive—each guest has a little present to open! Have someone help you so these can be prepared before the ice cream melts.

12 sheets colored tissue paper

12 pieces ribbon or rafia, or

   12 gold foil stickers

Confetti

Remove desserts from freezer one by one as you prepare them, but keep them in their plastic wrappers. Place a square of tissue paper on an individual plate or large serving tray. Gather up the ends to form a bundle at the top (shaped like a Hershey's Kiss). Twist to secure it and leave as is, or tie with ribbon, or stick with foil sticker. Sprinkle with confetti and serve.

"Dressed Up" Variation II

This is a little more like a real napoleon, with three layers, and very elegant.

Cookie recipe above, made
   with 1½ times the ingredients

Chocolate Sauce, and or
   Caramel Sauce
   (homemade or purchased)

1½ cups whipping cream

2 teaspoons vanilla
   (or coffee-flavored liqueur)

2 tablespoons sugar

Chocolate shavings or grated chocolate
   (shaved with knife or grated from
   dark, semi-sweet chocolate)

Mint leaves for garnish

Follow directions as above, but make half again as many cookies. (Or, if you like, make the same amount and make the cookies smaller, and cook 5 minutes less if you do.) When you go to make the sandwiches, spread layer of ice cream on top of first cookie. Layer another cookie on that, then another layer of ice cream, then another cookie. Wrap and freeze.

    When ready to serve, whip cream with vanilla (or liqueur) and sugar, and refrigerate. On large dinner plate, drizzle chocolate or caramel sauce (or both) in zig-zag or swirly designs, or two little pools. Unwrap the napoleon and place on top of the sauce. Top with a dollop of whipped cream and sprinkle with chocolate shavings or grated chocolate. Garnish with mint leaf.

Dinner in Highlands

*A*tlantans Hazel and Paul Sanger are known for their dinner parties. And when asked about these parties, their friends are known for shakes of the head and gleams in the eye. "Oh, the stories I could tell..."

When son Christopher turned 21, his parents surprised him with not just a dinner but an entire weekend of parties and picnics and barbecues, replete with family friends and school chums who flew in from all over. The group convened at the Sangers' weekend house in Highlands, North Carolina, a favorite getaway spot for Atlantans.

Following a hike through the mountains and a slightly precarious forging of the Chattooga River, the festivities began with a picnic on the riverbank. Paul had stayed behind at the house to prepare for the party that evening: a seated dinner for sixty, outdoors.

The extraordinary design for the house, completed in 1964, was inspired by the Metropolitan Opera set for the second act of Wagner's *Die Meistersinger*—the Hans Sachs house, to be exact. The land on which it stands was acquired by Paul's mother soon after the Second World War. The side lawn adjacent to the house forms a secluded alcove surrounded by rhododendron, native azalea, lilacs, hemlocks and towering white pines. Overlooking a naturalized, terraced garden that descends the mountain and leads into the forest, it was an ideal spot for dinner.

The dress was black tie and tennis shoes. Atlanta designer and friend John Oetgen lent a hand with the look of the party. He placed the six-foot-long tables end to end—"like a French wedding," he said—and alternated tablecloths, white with blue and white prints. Bess Finch saw to the flowers, which were loosely arranged and informal in simple glass vases. The candles were shielded by hurricane lanterns, and the votives held their own. Torches were placed in rows on either side of the table, and tiny white lights twinkled amid the peripheral greenery. Then just for fun, Oetgen spread the tabletop with white paper and put crayons at each place.

The dinner, an Italian feast served buffet-style from the dining table inside, was prepared in advance and transported from Atlanta by chef Candy Sheehan. Dessert was served from a table outside. And in a nostalgic nod to birthdays gone by, bubblegum—Bazooka in all flavors—was passed after coffee.

Our menu is a sort of Southwestern variation on Candy's classic Italian dishes, but she lent her advice and ideas to this version as well.

ENU

Spicy Breadsticks

Smoked Turkey and Black Bean Lasagne

Green Salad With Olive Oil and Lemon Juice

Vanilla Ice Cream With Coffee Liqueur and Toasted Coconut

Perfect Chocolate Cookies

SERVES 8

Spicy Breadsticks

As they warm, the breadsticks will absorb the flavor of the spices. You may want to experiment with these spices and the amounts. Test one or two before you do them all.

Storebought or bakery breadsticks
Olive oil
2 teaspoons chili powder

1 teaspoon salt (sea salt, if you have it)
1 teaspoon paprika

Spread breadsticks on a cookie sheet and very lightly brush with olive oil. Combine spices and sprinkle over breadsticks on cookie sheet. Cover loosely with foil and warm at 350° for about 10 minutes.

Paul and Hazel Sanger gave their son's twenty-first birthday party in the garden of their house in Highlands, North Carolina, a favorite getaway spot for Atlantans. Designer John Oetgen lined six-foot tables end to end and spread white paper atop for guests to color with crayons between courses.

Smoked Turkey and Black Bean Lasagne

This is my own recipe, and I use good smoked turkey from the deli, reduced fat Monterey Jack Cheese, nonfat ricotta, low fat cottage cheese, a medium spicy non-fat salsa, and whole-wheat lasagne noodles. It may also be halved and cooked in an 8 x 8 inch dish. And Candy passes on this hot tip: you do not need to pre-cook la-sagne noodles, ever. They cook in the sauce along with the rest of the dish.

2 cups tomato sauce	1 green pepper, diced
1 cup prepared salsa	1/4 cup fresh chopped cilantro
Lasagne noodles	8 ounces ricotta cheese
1 1/2 pounds smoked	8 ounces cottage cheese
turkey, diced	2 cups grated Monterey
2 (14-oz.) cans cooked black beans	Jack cheese

Dice turkey and green pepper, and chop cilantro. Heat oven to 350°. Rinse and drain beans, and add green pepper and cilantro. Set aside. Combine tomato sauce and salsa. Combine ricotta and cottage cheeses. In a 9 x 13-inch pan, spread 1 cup of the sauce, then one layer of (uncooked!) noodles, then another 1/2 cup of sauce. Next come layers of diced turkey, then bean mixture, Ricotta mixture, and Monterey Jack cheese. Begin again with pasta layer, 1/2 cup of sauce, turkey, etc., as before. Repeat once more. You should have a total of three pasta layers and end with the grated cheese. Cover with foil and bake for 35 minutes, then uncover and bake about 10 minutes more, so cheese is lightly brown and bubbly.

Green Salad With Olive Oil and Lemon Juice

Use mixed field greens, Bibb, Romaine, endive—an interesting mixture. Whisk to-gether (or shake up in a jar) 1/4 cup fresh lemon juice and 2/3 cups extra virgin olive oil, into which you add salt and pepper to taste, and a minced garlic clove or two, if you like.

Vanilla Ice Cream With Coffee Liqueur and Toasted Coconut

Courtesy Candy Sheehan, this is so simple and so divine. Also works with coconut or coffee ice cream, and with frozen yogurt.

Vanilla ice cream or frozen yogurt
1 cup shredded coconut

Coffee liqueur, such as Kahlua or
 Tia Maria

Spread coconut on cookie sheet and bake at 350° for 5 minutes, stir, and bake another minute or two. Watch it carefully; it doesn't take long. Or you may "toast" coconut in a skillet, as described on page 78. Scoop ice cream into bowls and pour over it a tablespoon or two of liqueur. Sprinkle with toasted coconut. Serve with Perfect Chocolate Cookies, shortbread, or by its own wonderful self.

Perfect Chocolate Cookies

This makes about 36 small cookies. Recipe can be doubled, and cookies freeze well.

2 squares chocolate, unsweetened
4 tablespoons butter
1 teaspoon instant coffee powder
 dissolved in 1 tablespoon hot water
1 cup sugar
1/2 teaspoon cinnamon

2 eggs
1 teaspoon vanilla
1 cup flour
1 teaspoon baking powder
1/2 teaspoon salt

In heavy saucepan or double boiler, melt butter and chocolate. Remove from heat and stir in coffee, sugar and cinnamon. Add eggs one at a time, beating well. Add vanilla. Sift together flour, baking powder and salt, and blend into chocolate. Cover with plastic wrap and chill for 2 hours or more. When ready to bake, heat oven to 375° and grease a cookie sheet. Scoop dough by half-teaspoonfuls and shape into balls. Bake about 10 minutes, and don't overbake. They should be soft when you take them out. Loosen from cookie sheet while still warm and remove to rack to cool.

A Southern Summer Wedding

*W*hen an Atlanta designer and her assistant set themselves to the task of said assistant's wedding, one charmed idea led to another, which eventually led the bride gracefully down the aisle, and then home, for her reception. "I don't think I considered having it anywhere else," recalls Ann Lanier Jackson, bride of Robert Brian Jackson. The idea of a home reception is certainly not exclusive to the South, but it does seem more prevalent here. Ties to family and tradition, a sense of history and pride of place remain strong in the South, and all are bound into the concept of home. It seems only fitting to celebrate one of life's most significant ceremonies amid the material shelter of one's own heritage.

"Home," before Ann came to Atlanta, was West Point, Georgia, about 90 miles from Atlanta, in a verdant valley run through by the Chattahoochee River and sustained largely by textile mills, the business in which Ann's family has been for five generations. The house's architecture and interiors bespeak strong French provincial affinities, but the garden and grounds are pure Georgia. It is in this combination of influences that Atlanta designer Susan Withers, with Ann, arrived at the idea of a French *orangerie*, but using our Southern materials to do it.

From the archives of Dan River Mills, in which Ann's father is a principal, came a lovely white and ecru toile to drape the tent and cover the tables and chairs. Atlanta floral designer Mary Jo Means brought in white crape myrtles as standards, created citrus tree topiaries, and fashioned centerpieces with white roses, in keeping with the overall aim for a feeling of coolness and shade. It was, after all, August. The effect was not just successful but stunning—elegance without ostentation, and an Atlanta creative team at its finest.

As to the menu, here is a sampling of appetizers and hors d'oeuvres sure to please (and impress) a crowd of 15 or 20, and suitable to be "dressed up" or "down," depending on the occasion. Any number of the other mostly do-ahead dishes in this volume would work for a large buffet as well—go scouting, particularly among the first courses. If you are the rare and courageous cook who might actually take on the food preparations for any reception of 50 or more, then you are a heartier soul than I, but I salute you.

 ## ＭＥＮＵ

Marinated Shrimp

Sumptuous Shredded Beef

Brie and Sundried Tomato Tart

Gingered Asparagus

SERVES 15 TO 20

Marinated Shrimp

3 pounds jumbo shrimp	1 medium onion, chopped in big pieces
2 tablespoons Dijon mustard	1 clove garlic, crushed
2 tablespoons grainy mustard	1 tablespoon thyme
2 tablespoons horseradish	$1/2$ teaspoon salt
$1\,1/4$ cups olive oil	$1/2$ teaspoon freshly ground black pepper
$2/3$ cup tarragon vinegar	$1/8$ teaspoon cayenne or red pepper

Place all ingredients except shrimp into blender or food processor, and process until smooth.

To cook shrimp, bring large pot of salted water to boil. Add shrimp and cook 3 minutes. Peel, keeping the tails intact, if you like. Place in large bowl and pour marinade over. Refrigerate until serving.

To serve, drain shrimp, reserving marinade, and place in bowl lined with lettuce leaves (if desired). Serve marinade on the side as a dip.

Sumptuous Shredded Beef

Simply the best of its kind, for any beef or venison, from North Carolina friend and ace cook, Hannah Dietrich. You can make this a day ahead. One of our testers added a tablespoon of French's mustard to the sauce and swore by it, but I think it's pretty darn good as is. Try the mustard in a bit of the sauce, if you like, and follow your preference.

3 ½ to 4 pounds chuck roast
  (or other roast or venison)
2 tablespoons flour
¼ cup Worcestershire sauce
¼ cup vinegar
3 tablespoons sugar
2 teaspoons chili powder

1 teaspoon salt
1 teaspoon dry mustard
1 teaspoon black pepper
⅛ teaspoon cayenne or red pepper
3 garlic cloves, minced
1 (14-ounce) bottle of ketchup

Heat oven to 300°. Sprinkle meat with flour and quickly brown in a roasting pan or Dutch oven with a little olive oil or butter. (Theoretically, browning seals the meat and therefore keeps it juicier, but for this recipe, you really can skip this step if you want to.) Combine remaining ingredients and pour over meat. Cook until it is falling apart, 1½ to 2 hours, depending on your oven and size of roast—in general allow about ½ hour per pound.

Remove from oven, shred meat, and return to pan. You may need to add a little water. Serve in a chafing dish with rolls on the side.

Brie and Sundried Tomato Tart

I realize these ingredients border on the passé, but it's food, not a fashion show. When everybody loves it, why not? I list the ingredients for one tart only here. For a crowd, double it and make two.

Atlantans seem to have an affinity for French provincial style, as is fluently expressed by designer Susan Withers in this tented reception at home for bride Ann Lanier Jackson. Mary Jo Means created the topiaries of flowers, fresh herbs, and citrus.

Pastry crust for 1 (10-inch) tart
  or quiche pan
Quiche dishes or tart pan
  with removable sides
8 ounces brie cheese, rind
  removed and cut into small pieces
¾ cup milk (low fat OK)

¼ cup chopped sundried tomatoes
  (already packed in oil or,
  if dried, soaked in boiling water
  for 15 minutes and drained)
¼ cup fresh chopped basil
3 eggs
2 tablespoons grated Parmesan cheese

In a 10-inch tart or quiche pan, partially bake the pastry shell for 8 minutes at 400°. Let it cool while you prepare remaining ingredients.

Reduce oven heat to 350°. Place brie in bottom of tart, then place sundried tomatoes on top. Sprinkle with basil. Beat eggs and milk together until frothy, and pour over all. Sprinkle with Parmesan cheese. Bake 45 minutes or until golden on top and middle is set. Let cool before cutting.

Gingered Asparagus

This is so simple I almost cannot understand why it is so good. But it is. I guess some of the best things are. Good over any steamed vegetables, by the way. If you're making for a crowd, double it. Two pounds of asparagus will serve 8 as a side dish; four pounds will easily take care of 15 to 20 for hors d'oeuvres. Allow at least an hour for asparagus to marinate.

2 pounds asparagus
1 tablespoon butter
1 clove garlic, crushed
1 heaping tablespoon grated fresh ginger
1/3 cup vegetable or chicken stock
1/4 cup olive oil

1/4 cup fresh lemon juice
2 tablespoons soy sauce
1 medium tomato, peeled, seeded and diced
1/4 cup finely chopped scallions

In small saucepan over medium-low heat, melt butter and sauté garlic and ginger just until garlic begins to turn light golden. Remove from heat and whisk in remaining ingredients except oil. Then, whisking constantly, add oil in a steady stream. Pour over asparagus and let marinate an hour or two.

Veneralia

From what its brochure calls "humble beginnings as a collection of miscellanea in the 1870s," a certain art and archaeology museum in Atlanta is today a nationally acclaimed institution whose antiquities and fine arts collections are of the first calibre. In 1919, four years after Emory College in Oxford, Georgia, was established in Atlanta as Emory University, a group of professors founded the Emory University Museum—the first art museum in the city. That museum is today known as the Michael C. Carlos Museum, in honor of the Atlanta businessman whose generosity has both permitted and encouraged the museum's phenomenal growth.

Originally housed in one of the oldest buildings on campus, a 1916 Beaux Arts design by well-known New York architect Henry Hornbostle, the museum underwent major renovation in 1985 and grand expansion in 1993. Both phases are the work of architect and designer Michael Graves, whose elegantly simple postmodernism is deemed the ideal complement to the treasures and relics of ancient cultures of Greece, Rome, Egypt, the Near East, Latin America, Africa, and to a lesser extent, North America and Asia. Augmenting the museum's offerings are growing fine arts collections ranging from Middle Ages to Renaissance works on paper to prints and photographs from the nineteenth and twentieth centuries.

Part of what keeps this and any museum going, of course, is private contributions, sometimes solicited in the form of lovely and imaginative invitations to fabulous fund-raisers—equally lovely and imaginative, and occasionally almost breathtaking. The Carlos Museum's "Veneralia" is such an event, revived after the ancient Roman festival of Venus, wherein women would bathe in the men's baths in hopes that their affairs of the heart might be favored. In addition to celebrating the goddess Venus, women, according to their rank, offered incense to Fortuna Virilis and paid homage to the wind gods. In the modern-day Emory version—the first in thousands of years and no doubt the first in which tuxedos and ball gowns were worn—the theme of the Veneralia was carried out to the hilt.

Centerpiece of the 1993 ball was a magnificent wooden replica of "The Tower of the Winds," an octagonal marble building in Athens dating from the first century B.C. A creative committee led by Susan Withers and David Heath organized more than forty Atlanta architects, artists and designers to interpret the theme in the form of more than forty individual centerpieces and tablescapes. The results were extraordinary, and the scene of the ballroom under a beautiful tent on the campus quadrangle most certainly would have inspired Venus herself. Ball chairmen were Jean Astrop, Roya Irvani and Ginny Millner.

As the Veneralia is an early springtime event, our menu is somewhat light but completely scrumptuous and assuredly easy. It even includes whipped potatoes, arguably a "windblown" sort of food. The idea for this divine repast comes from Atlantan Alex Hitz, an accomplished cook and entertainer, and a dear friend.

ENU

Spinach Salad With Pine Nuts, Apples and Bacon

Seared Salmon With Mashed Potatoes And Dilled Shallot Sauce

Steamed Asparagus

Meringues With Sherbert and Raspberry Sauce

SERVES 6

I don't know what it is about mashed potatoes, but I think you could serve them with boiled tennis shoes and people would still rave about the meal. So imagine how they rave over this dinner, and enjoy it. If you want to simplify, serve the spinach and dressing without the pine nuts, etc., or omit it, since you are having asparagus with the meal anyway. Or you could have the salad and omit the asparagus. For the dessert, omit the meringues and serve the sherbert with raspberry sauce and some good biscotti or cookies.

The extravagant "Veneralia" is a fund-raiser for the Michael C. Carlos Museum of art and archaeology at Emory University. The party is named for the ancient Roman festival of Venus, and in this particular year, each table was decorated by a different Atlanta artist, architect or designer.

Spinach Salad With Pine Nuts, Apples and Bacon

Dressing
$1/3$ cup olive oil

2 tablespoons white wine vinegar

2 teaspoons Dijon mustard

1 teaspoon soy sauce

$1/2$ teaspoon curry powder

$1/2$ teaspoon sugar

Salt and freshly ground pepper

Salad
$3/4$ pound spinach, stems removed, leaves washed, dried and torn into pieces

$1/2$ cup green apple, diced

6 pieces bacon, cooked and crumbled

$1/4$ cup pine nuts, toasted

Put all dressing ingredients in a jar and shake. Pour in bottom of salad bowl. Place spinach in bowl on top of dressing, then apples and bacon on top of that, but do not toss. Cover and refrigerate until ready to serve, then toss and sprinkle with toasted pine nuts.

Seared Salmon

Since the fish only takes a few minutes to cook, try to cook it at the last minute. If you must do ahead, try to do it no more than 30 minutes before serving, and put fish aside on a plate, uncovered. If you need to reheat it, cover loosely with foil and warm for 10 to 15 minutes in a 350° oven, but know that it will cook a bit more in the process and adjust your initial cooking time if necessary.

⅓ cup olive oil
Salt and freshly ground pepper

6 salmon filets, about 6 ounces each
Fresh parsley and dill for garnish

Rub salmon with olive oil and sprinkle with salt and pepper. Marinate at least half an hour, and turn to coat all sides. In skillet sprayed with nonstick spray, over medium-high to high heat, sear (brown) salmon on both sides, about 2 minutes per side. Then lower heat to medium, cover and cook another 2 minutes per side, depending upon thickness of filet. To serve, place salmon on bed of Mashed Potatoes and serve with Dilled Shallot Sauce. Sprinkle all over salmon and plate with fresh parsley and dill.

Dilled Shallot Sauce

One of the beauties of this very special sauce, besides its sublime taste, is that it can be made ahead, refrigerated, and re-heated before serving.

6 tablespoons (¾ stick) butter
½ cup vermouth
½ cup fish stock* (chicken stock OK)
3 tablespoons fresh chopped dill

½ to ¾ cup (4 to 6 ounces) stemmed
   and chopped mushrooms,
   preferably shiitake, but any will do
¼ cup chopped shallots

*No, I do not always have freshly made stock on hand. I use bouillon cubes of the Knorr brand to make stock—fish, chicken, and beef.

In a saucepan over medium-high heat, melt butter, vermouth and stock together and sauté mushrooms and shallots. Cook for about 6 to 8 minutes, or until reduced by about one fourth and slightly thickened. At this point you may either remove from heat until ready to serve, or lower heat and continue.

Stir in 1 tablespoon of the dill. Spoon sauce over salmon and potatoes and sprinkle remaining dill over all. If you prefer to serve the sauce on the side—that famous first line in the Battle Hymn of the Reducing—sprinkle the dill on top of the salmon and potatoes as they are. (And if someone doesn't want the sauce, for heaven's sake, have a few big lemon wedges on hand.)

Mashed Potatoes I

This version is slightly denser and richer than the second version, on page 37. Your preference, or use what you have on hand.

1 1/2 pounds russet or baking potatoes, peeled and cut into 1 1/2- to 2-inch chunks

2 tablespoons milk (skim milk OK)

4 tablespoons butter (optional, but if omitting, add 1/4 cup more milk)

4 ounces light cream cheese, or Neufchatel cream cheese (regular cream cheese OK)

1 teaspoon each salt and freshly ground pepper, or to taste

1/4 teaspoon paprika

2 tablespoons Parmesan cheese

Place potatoes in large pot. Add salted water to cover, and bring to boil. Reduce heat and cook until potatoes are tender, about 25 minutes. Meanwhile, warm milk and butter together. (No, you don't *have* to, it just helps the potatoes stay hotter longer.) Drain and mash potatoes by hand or put through a food mill. Whip in milk, butter (if using) and cream cheese, and season to taste. If you are making ahead, put in a casserole dish, sprinkle with the Parmesan cheese, and cover. When ready to serve, warm 10 to 15 minutes at 350°.

Mashed Potatoes II

1½ pounds potatoes (as above)
1 cup buttermilk
2 tablespoons butter

1 teaspoon each salt and freshly
    ground pepper
¼ teaspoon paprika
2 tablespoons Parmesan cheese

Follow directions as for version I, on page 36.

Steamed Asparagus

1½ pounds asparagus
Olive oil and/or butter

Lemon juice
Salt

Steam, boil or microwave asparagus until crisp tender. Toss with a tablespoon of olive oil and/or butter and a little lemon juice. Salt to taste.

Meringues With Sherbert and Raspberry Sauce

Meringues

Meringues always elicit such oohs and ahs that people simply assume they are diffi-cult to make. Pooh. Couldn't be easier. Just don't make them on an extra humid or rainy day, or they'll be sticky.

3 egg whites, at room temperature
¾ cup sugar
1 teaspoon vanilla

⅛ teaspoon almond extract or anise
    flavoring (optional)

Grease a baking sheet and heat oven to 225°. Beat whites until frothy. Continue to beat, adding sugar slowly, about a tablespoon at a time. Add vanilla and anise, if using. Mixture should hold stiff peaks. Place 6 large spoonfuls on baking sheet. Using the back of a spoon, form into round shells. Bake about an hour and 15 minutes, and turn off the oven. Crack the oven door and let the meringues cool completely in the oven.

Sherberts

Raspberry, lemon, or peach sherberts or sorbets, ice creams or frozen yogurts, or combination

Fresh mint leaves for garnish

Raspberry Sauce

This is just as good made with strawberries or blueberries, and good to have on hand for a last-minute dessert—with fresh berries or fruit and angelfood cake, for example.

2 packages frozen raspberries or strawberries, in light syrup
1 tablespoon fresh lemon juice

1-2 tablespoons cassis or framboise (optional)

Thaw berries and puree in food processor. Add lemon juice and liqueur. If the raspberry seeds bother you, strain them out. Will keep for a week in the refrigerator.

TO ASSEMBLE
Scoop sherbert or sorbet into meringue shells, bowls or parfait glasses. Pour sauce over or pass separately. Garnish with sprigs of fresh mint.

Tailgating at the Steeplechase

*T*ailgating is not strictly a Southern tradition, but it does seem to flourish here, perhaps because of the warm weather, the fondness for outdoor events—sporting and otherwise—and the sort of convivial, relaxed hospitality it fosters and for which the South is reputed.

The South's reputation for equestrian pursuits is more obscure, however, and Atlanta's equestrian heritage in particular is pretty low on the city's claims to fame, competing as it must with everything from the Braves, to *Gone With the Wind*, to CNN. But it exists, nonetheless, and the nearby communities of Alpharetta, Conyers, Newnan and others have become quite the horsey enclaves.

While the rarefied worlds of fox-hunting, show-jumping and the like may be perquisites for the elite, the steeplechase is very much a spectator sport, where watching the people is as interesting and unpredictable as watching the horses. The printed program even includes several pages of humorous anecdotes accumulated over the years. To wit: Veteran steeplechase steward Tom Martin recalls one day when he ran to the aid of a just-unseated jockey. Martin asked if he was all right, and the jockey said yes. "Do you need a doctor?" Martin persisted. "Yes," the young man replied, "a psychiatrist!" Another longtime patron, Ginny Hobbs, claims not to have known that "there were horses running around the field" until after her third year in attendance. I swear.

Indeed, horses have been running around the field since March of 1966, at the first officially sanctioned Atlanta Hunt Meeting and Steeplechase. For the next five years, they galloped along the loamy banks of the Chattahoochee, on farm land belonging to the Wayt family of Atlanta. The chase then moved north to Cumming, Georgia, again on Wayt land, where it continued to attract ever larger crowds and corporate sponsorships. Then, the state department of transportation decided it needed a highway right through those fields, and the steeplechase was out of business—at that site, anyway. But not for good. This "racy" rite of spring will go on as always, at a newly built course on the Floyd-Bartow County line, in a bend of the Etowah River, near Rome, Georgia. And again, as always since 1976, the Atlanta Speech School will benefit from funds raised for the event.

The "at table" aspect of the Atlanta Steeplechase takes many forms—from grand catered affairs under elegantly appointed tents, to pimiento cheese sandwiches on the tailgate of a truck. My menu here is more along tailgating lines, and truthfully, several of the other menus in this book would work as well. Just don't leave out the brownies. Something about tailgating simply calls out for brownies. I think it's a law. The same statute applies to pimiento cheese sandwiches, but it is not enforced as rigorously.

ENU

Avocado and Bacon Sandwiches

Vitello Tonnato

Green Rice Salad

Herbed Cherry Tomatoes

Best Ever Brownies

SERVES 4

This is a good menu, and not one you see everyday—though you might after word gets around about how wonderful yours was. To streamline it, forget the hors d'oeuvre and have cheese straws. Also, forget the Herbed Cherry Tomatoes and serve plain sliced tomatoes. The rice is easy and good. It is also good with the Tonnato sauce, as the two will inevitably interact with the meat. Fresh fruit would be good for the dessert if you want to pass on the brownies. But I bet you won't.

The Atlanta Steeplechase is an annual rite of spring and a tour-de-force tailgating event.

Avocado and Bacon Sandwiches

These are just perfect, thanks to Alex Hitz. But if you're in the mood to overdo it, add a thin slice of fresh plum tomato and a few leaves of watercress just before serving. Otherwise they can be made several hours ahead. The English butter their bread to keep the sandwiches from becoming soggy. That isn't really necessary here, but it's good.

1 large ripe avocado
2 tablespoons mayonnaise
1 tablespoon minced red onion
2 teaspoons fresh lemon juice
½ teaspoon Worcestershire sauce

1 loaf very thinly sliced white
   or wheat bread
2 tablespoons butter, softened (optional)
5 pieces bacon, crisply cooked
   and broken into small bite-size pieces

Halve the avocado; remove and reserve the pit. Scoop out flesh into bowl. Use a fork or food processor to blend in remaining ingredients except bacon. Place pit into mixture to keep avocado from turning brown. Cover and refrigerate, or serve immediately as follows: Use round cookie cutter to cut the bread for the sandwiches. If you like, lightly butter the rounds. Spread with avocado mixture and top with a piece or two of bacon. Top with another piece of bread or leave them open-faced. If making ahead, do them close-faced, cover with a damp paper towel, store in an air-tight container, and refrigerate.

Vitello Tonnato

I have generally avoided foreign recipe titles, but somehow "Vitello Tonnato" sounds so much more elegant—not to mention appetizing—than "Veal With Tuna Sauce," which is what it is. I was afraid it might turn people off, but please, please don't pass this by. It is a quickie version of an Italian classic, and it is a divine combination of flavors. Besides, you don't often see it served in this country, and you do want to be different, don't you? Can be made with veal, chicken or turkey. If you have homemade mayonnaise on hand or are inclined to make it, do so by all means. I admit it is better—but this version is still very good.

¾ cup mayonnaise
   (homemade would be great;
   reduced fat OK, too)
1 can (about 6 ounces) tuna
   packed in oil, drained
6 anchovy filets, chopped
1 tablespoon fresh lemon juice
   plus extra lemon slices
   for garnish
2 tablespoons olive oil
Salt and freshly ground pepper

8 to 12 slices cold roasted veal,
   or chicken or turkey breasts
   (if using chicken breasts,
   pound them to just under a
   half-inch thickness,
   and poach or sauté them.)
1 small head Bibb (or other)
   lettuce, for garnish
2 medium tomatoes, sliced,
   for garnish*
2 tablespoons capers, drained

Combine mayonnaise, tuna, anchovies in blender or food processor. (If you're making the rice salad afterwards, don't wash the food processor because you'll be using it again; do rinse it out, however.) Add half the lemon juice and olive oil and check consistency. It should be creamy and smooth. Add more lemon juice and oil if necessary. Salt and pepper to taste.

Arrange lettuce leaves on plate, then veal, chicken or turkey, and pour sauce over. Garnish with lemon slices, tomatoes (if you use them) and capers.

*If you make the Herbed Cherry Tomatoes, omit the tomatoes in the garnish.

Green Rice Salad

Just-cooked and still-warm rice absorbs the dressing better.

½ cup cold, cooked spinach, chopped
⅔ cup vinaigrette dressing
   (prepared or using recipe
   on page 14)

2 cups rice, still warm from cooking
½ cup artichoke hearts, chopped
   (optional)
¼ cup pine nuts, toasted (optional)

In blender or processor, blend spinach and vinaigrette dressing. Begin by pouring half of the mixture into the rice, and add more to taste. Serve as is or add the artichokes and pine nuts, if you like.

Herbed Cherry Tomatoes

1 pint basket cherry tomatoes,
cut in half; or 7 or 8 plum tomatoes,
cut in thick slices

1 tablespoon olive oil or
on-hand vinaigrette dressing

2 tablespoons fresh herbs—
any combination of parsley,
chervil, chives, tarragon, basil

Salt and freshly ground pepper

Toss all ingredients together. Salt and pepper to taste.

Best Ever Brownies

So moist and chocolatey, with a thin layer of caramel and nuts in the middle. If you are in a hurry, you can make this with a prepared brownie mix and follow the instructions as they are here for the caramel and nuts.

½ cup (1 stick) of butter

2 ounces semisweet chocolate

4 ounces unsweetened chocolate

1 cup brown sugar, packed

¾ cup granulated sugar

1½ teaspoons vanilla

⅛ teaspoons cinnamon

1⅓ cups sifted flour

2 teaspoons baking powder

1¼ teaspoons salt

4 eggs

1 8-ounce package caramels

1 5-ounce can of evaporated milk

¾ cup chopped pecans

Grease a 9 x 13-inch pan. Heat oven to 350°. In heavy saucepan (large enough to hold all ingredients except caramels), over low heat, melt butter and chocolate. Remove from heat and stir in sugars, vanilla and cinnamon. Mix in flour, baking powder and salt. Add eggs one at a time, beating after each. Pour half the mixture into the pan and bake for 7 minutes. While it is baking, melt caramels in double boiler or microwave, and stir in milk until well blended. After 7 minutes, remove the partially baked brownies from the oven and drizzle with the caramel, then sprinkle with the nuts. Pour or spoon remaining brownie mix over, and bake another 30 to 35 minutes. These are very gooey. Best to refrigerate before cutting—if you can wait that long.

A Juneteenth Celebration

Atlanta's African-American community is a vibrant and substantive force shaping the city's political, social and cultural scenes. In the arts especially, Atlanta abounds with theatre, dance and music groups, and a few special performance venues. The National Black Arts Festival, begun in 1988 and co-chaired that year by Harry Belafonte and Cicely Tyson, is the only one of its kind in the country, if not the world. Held biennially in late summer, the festival hosts internationally renowned artists and performers as well as new and developing talent for a week of revelry and show.

There are other African-American festivals, too, not original to Atlanta but still relatively young in their histories. Kwanza is one, based on a traditional African harvest festival and held during, but not necessarily exclusive of, the Christmas and Hannukah time of year. Another, perhaps lesser-known, but catching-on, holiday is called "Juneteenth."

It sometimes slips the memory of history that not all members of the British American colonies celebrate their independence on July 4. For slaves, it was not until Abraham Lincoln's Emancipation Proclamation took effect some 87 years later, on New Year's Day in 1863. But for slaves in Texas, freedom came later still—more than two years later. On June 19, 1865, by order of Major-General Gordon Granger, "The people are informed that, in accordance with a proclamation from the Executive of the United States, all slaves are free . . ." And so it was printed the following day in the *Galveston Tri-weekly News*, giving rise to days of celebration thereafter. The festivities, both public and private, have since spread to other states, Georgia among them, fixing Juneteenth in the heart of Atlanta's summertime rituals.

It is a day for gatherings of families and friends, in the back yard or on the patio, or anywhere that lends itself to casual entertaining. Amid the tall pines holding sway over the rolling hills of Cascade Heights, the southwest Atlanta home of Lt. Col. and Mrs. Charles W. Dryden is an ideal setting. And the Drydens are especially appropriate hosts. Charles was one of an elite few to break a formidable

49

color barrier in the United States military when he joined the famous "Tuskegee Airmen," an all-black fighter squadron in World War II which flew missions over Europe and North Africa. Mrs. Dryden—Marymal—was for years a teacher of the Atlanta University School of Social Work (now Clark-Atlanta University).

Like the Drydens' story, Juneteenth is about pride of heritage. As a special occasion, the festive meal might be anything from a simple barbeque to a glorious, traditional feast—or, like we have here, something in between. The Drydens' fare was prepared by Marymal and her friend Geneva Francais. A graduate of the Cordon Bleu, Geneva says her cooking combines French technique with African spice.

Our menu departs from the Drydens' original, copious spread, but it does incorporate elements of traditional Southern cuisine, with a deviation or two for flavorful fun.

$\mathcal{M}$ENU

Roasted Summer Vegetable Terrine

Grilled Pork Tenderloin on Creamy Cheese Grits

Baby Lima Beans

Peach Cobbler

SERVES 6 TO 8

If the summer tomatoes are really good, definitely have them fresh, sliced, with a dab of homemade mayonnaise. There's nothing better. If they are not especially good at the moment, Herbed Cherry Tomatoes on page 47 would be another option. If you do have tomatoes elsewhere, you might want to eliminate them from the vegetable terrine and substitute roasted red peppers, which you can roast yourself or buy prepared. To streamline: You may certainly omit either the terrine or the lima beans and have a gorgeous summer meal. Have fresh peaches and cookies or watermelon for dessert, or some of those storebought popsicles made from fruit.

Roasted Summer Vegetable Terrine

This is an easy and versatile dish good with almost any grilled or roasted meats, or by itself with good bread and a green salad. You can do ahead and re-heat, or serve room temperature or cold. If you're having tomatoes elsewhere, adjust this recipe by substituting roasted red peppers (page 13) for the tomatoes. You may also add a pound of sliced mozarella cheese, layered in the middle and on top.

2 medium eggplants,
   peeled and sliced lengthwise
   $1/4$ inch thick
6 to 8 medium zucchini,
   trimmed and sliced lengthwise
   $1/4$ inch thick
$1/3$ cup olive oil

Salt and freshly ground pepper
2 tablespoons tomato sauce
8 to 10 medium tomatoes, thinly sliced
$1/2$ cup fresh basil which has been cut
   into thin strips
4 to 6 garlic cloves, minced
Salt and freshly ground pepper

Prepare all ingredients first and the assembly will be quick. Heat oven to 450°. Rub a little of the oil on 1 or 2 baking sheets. Lay the eggplant and zucchini in a single layer on the sheets and brush lightly with olive oil, and sprinkle with salt and pepper. Roast for about 10 to 12 minutes, until cooked through and barely browned. You may have to roast the vegetables in shifts. Let the vegetables cool, and lower the oven heat to 350°. Mix together the basil and garlic. Spread the tomato sauce in the bottom of a 9 x 13-inch baking dish. Layer half the eggplant, then zucchini, then tomatoes. Sprinkle with salt and pepper and half the basil-garlic mixture. Repeat layers and cover with foil. Bake 20 to 25 minutes. Uncover and let cool for a few minutes before cutting into squares to serve. If you want a true "terrine" effect, take the foil used during baking and spread directly on top of vegetables, then weight down with heavy books or other objects for several hours and serve at room temperature or cold.

Grilled Pork Tenderloin

These ingredients are unusual, but the first taste will leave you swooning. A crust is formed by searing the meat first, further enhancing this dish's texture and flavor. I like adding half a cup of grainy mustard to the marinade, but that's up to you. Served over creamy cheese grits, it is Southern food, courtesy Alex Hitz, at its most sublime. Allow time to marinate several hours or overnight.

3 pounds (give or take) pork tenderloin
1 tablespoon dried thyme
2 teaspoons each salt and
   freshly ground pepper

1 cup honey melted with
   2 tablespoons butter
½ cup grainy mustard (optional)
1 small can (6 ounces)
   apple juice concentrate, thawed

Rub entire loin (or loins) with salt, pepper and thyme. Combine remaining ingredients in sealable plastic bag or shallow baking dish, add pork, and marinate overnight. If cooking on grill, sear meat over high heat first then over lower heat to finish cooking. Total time should be about 45 minutes to 1 hour, or until inside is barely still pink. If cooking in oven, broil for 5 to 10 minutes, then lower heat to 325° and roast 40 to 50 minutes, until done.

Creamy Cheese Grits

3 tablespoons butter

1 clove garlic, crushed

2 cups plus ½ cup milk,
   plus a little extra to add
   during cooking, if necessary

2 cups water

1 teaspoon salt

1 cup regular (not instant) grits

1¾ cups grated sharp chedder cheese,
   divided into 1 ½ cups and ¼ cup

⅓ cup grated Parmesan cheese

¼ teaspoon cayenne pepper

Dash of Worcestershire sauce

3 eggs, lightly beaten

Butter a 2-quart casserole with 1 tablespoon of the butter, and rub the sides of the dish with the garlic, leaving the garlic in the dish. Cook grits according to package directions, which will take anywhere from 20 to 35 minutes. Add more milk if grits get too thick too soon, but no more than ¼ cup. Heat oven to 350°. When grits are cooked, stir in ½ cup milk and all remaining ingredients except ¼ cup cheddar cheese. Pour into casserole and sprinkle with remaining ¼ cup cheese and bake, covered, for 45 minutes. Uncover and bake another 15 minutes.

Baby Lima Beans

If you're lucky enough to come across fresh butterbeans or baby lima beans, by all means use those. Frozen beans are quite satisfactory these days, however, and the method of flash-freezing them ensures retention of nutrients and fresh flavor. I find cooking them in chicken stock seasons them perfectly and they don't need butter.

2 or 3 (10-ounce) packages
frozen baby limas, with
no butter added

Chicken stock for cooking
(fresh or from bouillon cubes)
Freshly ground pepper

Cook according to package directions, and be sure not to overcook. They should be tender but still firm to the tooth. Frozen beans take 10 to 20 minutes.

Peach Cobbler

This recipe is so good and so simple. Use with other fruits—blackberries or blueberries, if you like, or even pears in the fall. Or change the spice to cardamom, cinnamon or ginger, but go lightly.

3 cups sliced peaches

1 cup sugar, divided

1/4 teaspoon mace

1/2 stick butter

1 cup flour

1 teaspoon baking powder

1 cup milk

Vanilla ice cream or
 frozen yogurt, if desired

Cinnamon, if desired

Heat oven to 350°. Sprinkle peaches with mace and 1/4 cup sugar. (Use more sugar if you think you need it.) Put butter in baking dish and melt it in the oven, being careful not to brown or burn it. Set aside. In another bowl, combine remaining sugar, flour and baking powder, then stir in the milk. Pour this into the baking dish, on top of the butter. Then spoon in the fruit. Bake 1 hour. Serve with vanilla ice cream or frozen yogurt, sprinkled with just a hint of cinnamon.

A Taste of Thai

*A*tlanta's ethnic diversity and multiculturalism have become a point of pride for the city and a magnet for the international community as well, culturally and commercially. Atlanta's increasingly cosmopolitan cachet on the one hand and its vibrant multicultural influences on the other no doubt have contributed to the city's hosting the 1996 Olympic Games. From Western Europe, to the Middle East, to Latin America, to the Pacific Rim, a great many of the world's regions are represented here, and their presence lends richness and energy to what, incredibly, was once a sleepy and provincial Southern city.

Their presence also lends great variety to the restaurant scene in Atlanta, with respect to Asian restaurants, especially. That may be due in part to the fact that Atlanta's Asian communities are the fastest growing populations in Atlanta, with Chinese, Korean, Thai, Filipino, Vietnamese and other Southeast Asian countries represented here. Atlanta food critic Terrell Vermont said that restaurants along Buford Highway—a non-descript, urban-sprawled strip of car dealers, fast-food chains, shopping centers and stop lights—"offer some of the best Asian cuisine served in America, and it is possible to walk into establishments where very little English is spoken. You may think you're in a Hong Kong dim sum house, or in a noodle soup emporium in Vietnam, or in a Japanese yakitori house. If it's authentic fare you're after, Atlanta fits the bill." That is how Terrell summed it up in her introduction to *The Unofficial Guide to Dining in Atlanta,* first published in 1994.

Terrell was a food critic for *Atlanta Magazine,* the newsletter *Knife and Fork,* a contributor to *The New York Times Magazine* and *Veranda,* among others. She was also the author of *Best of Vietnamese Cooking* (Centurion) and co-author, with Eve Zibart and Muriel Stevens, of *The Unofficial Guide to Ethnic Cuisine and Dining in America,* published in 1995 by Macmillan. Not only did Terrell study the cuisines of countries all over the world, but she learned in the kitchens of her friends and associates who live there. She had a particular affinity for Asia, as well as a penchant for Asian food, and she had a marvelous way of de-mystifying the recipes and their sometimes unusual components. Her Thai feast, here, won some of the biggest raves from our test kitchens, especially from the amateurs (and from me) who might

57

otherwise have skipped this kind of menu since it calls for a few special ingredients and perhaps a trip to an Asian food market. But believe me, it is well, well worth it, and easy to prepare.

As this book was being prepared in January of 1996, Terrell died of cancer. Aside from being an outright character and a wonderful wit, she was a gifted writer and a great spirit. Atlanta and her many friends will sorely miss her.

*M*ENU

Lemon Grass Soup With Shrimp

Aromatic Seafood Salad

Minced Chicken Salad

Red Curry With Beef

Green Beans With Sesame Seeds and Ginger

Jasmine Rice

Fresh Fruit

Coconut Macaroons

SERVES 6 TO 8

This is a copious offering, but fun for the array of flavors it offers. All can be prepared ahead and served slightly chilled or at room temperature, except the soup. If you prepare the soup ahead, remove it from the heat as soon as it is cooked and refrigerate it. Then gently re-heat at serving time. Do not over-cook the shrimp or they will be mushy. The rice shouldn't sit around for more than an hour, but since you don't have to watch it, it is easy enough to prepare just before serving time. If you want the macaroons but don't want to make them, most bakeries have them on hand. As to the special ingredients: This is one of the few places in this book where I deviate from my you-can-buy-it-at-any-small-town-grocery rule. Fish sauce, curry paste, unsweetened coconut milk, lemon grass and jasmine rice can be purchased at Asian markets and some specialty food stores. If you cannot find, phone a specialty food store and inquire about mail-order sources. Or, phone a Thai or Asian restaurant and sweetly inquire what you might buy from them. To streamline: A lovely meal would be the soup, any one or two of the main courses, the beans and rice, and fresh fruit.

Lemon Grass Soup With Shrimp

6 cups seafood stock
   (If you make the Aromatic
   Seafood Salad, save the
   poaching liquid and use for this.
   You could also substitute
   3 cups chicken stock
   and 3 cups clam juice.)
4 stalks lemon grass
1 pound fresh raw shrimp,
   shelled and de-veined

1/4 cup fresh cilantro, chopped
2 tablespoons fish sauce
Juice of 2 limes
Pinch of sugar
2 green onions, white and green
   parts, finely minced
1 hot pepper, finely minced
   (or more, if you like it hot)

Measure and prepare all ingredients in advance. In large pot, heat stock, and add lemon grass and shrimp. When shrimp are just beginnning to turn pink, add remaining ingredients. Taste and, if necessary, add more fish sauce or lime juice to achieve a nice, tart taste. Garnish with minced green onion and hot pepper.

Aromatic Seafood Salad

1 pound cleaned squid (or other seafood—shrimp, scallops, crab or firm, white fish, or combination thereof)	3 tablespoons lime juice
	2 teaspoons minced hot peppers, or more, to taste
	1 teaspoon sugar, or more to taste
2 green onions, white and green parts minced	1 cup mint leaves
2 tablespoons fish sauce	1/3 cup basil leaves (purple basil, if you can find it)

Poach squid (or other seafood) one minute. Drain and place in bowl. (Save liquid to make soup, above.) To begin seasoning, add 1 tablespoon each of fish sauce and lime juice. Add minced peppers and sugar. Increase in small amounts to taste. (I usually end up using 2 tablespoons fish sauce, 3 tablespoons lime juice, 2 teaspoons minced hot peppers, 1 teaspoon sugar.) Add herbs and serve.

Minced Chicken Salad

Serve this on a bed of lettuce.

1 chicken, boiled, skinned, boned and minced, or use already skinned and boned breasts (3 to 3 1/2 cups total)	1/2 cup fresh mint
	1 red onion, thinly sliced
	1/4 cup uncooked rice
1/2 cup fresh cilantro	2 tablespoons fish sauce
	2 tablespoons lime juice

In large bowl, combine chicken, herbs and onion. In dry frying pan over medium heat, "toast" the rice, shaking and stirring carefully so as not to burn it, 5-7 minutes. When it is golden, remove to a mortar and pestle or food processor and crack sightly. Add to chicken mixture and season with fish sauce and lime juice.

Red Curry With Beef

This would also be good over noodles.

1 can (4 ounces) red
   curry paste (Panaeng curry)
2 cups coconut milk

1 pound flank steak or London broil,
   cut in 1/4-inch thick slices

In large pot, heat curry paste and stir-fry for 2 minutes over medium heat. (If it is sticking to the pan add a teaspoon or two of oil.) Lower heat, add beef and coconut milk. Cover and cook about 1½ to 2 hours or until beef is tender. Skim fat occasionally, while cooking—but there won't be much.

Green Beans With Sesame Seeds and Ginger

2 pounds green beans
1/4 cup sesame seeds
   (buy in bulk at a health food store)
3 tablespoons olive oil

2 tablespoons fresh lemon juice
1 teaspoon grated fresh ginger
Pinch of red pepper flakes

To toast the sesame seeds, spread in a dry skillet on the stove. Cook over medium heat, stirring often, until golden brown—about 7 minutes. Bring a large pot of water to boil, add a teaspoon or two of salt, then add beans, cooking 3 to 5 minutes, until crisp-tender. Pour into a collander and run cold water over to stop the cooking. (Or dump ice water over them.) Combine remaining ingredients and toss with the beans and sesame seeds. Refrigerate if making in advance, but serve at room temperature. For a variation, add a teaspoon or so of crushed, fresh garlic, or a teaspoon of soy sauce.

Popular food writer and accomplished cook Terrell Vermont.

Jasmine Rice

4 cups water   2 cups jasmine rice

The preferred way of cooking jasmine rice is to steam it, but if you do not have a steamer, bring 4 cups of water to a boil, add the rice, stir and reduce heat to simmer. Cover and forget about it for the next 40 minutes. Then remove from heat and fluff with a fork. Cover again until serving time—but don't wait more than an hour.

Fresh Fruit

Choose melons, pineapples or strawberries. Take your pick or use all three. Serve in hollowed-out pineapple or melon halves—or in a basket carved from a whole watermelon.

Coconut Macaroons

2 cups flaked, sweetened coconut

2 egg whites, lightly beaten

$1/4$ cup sweetened condensed milk

1 teaspoon vanilla

Heat oven to 350°. Grease a cookie sheet and set aside. Toast coconut by spreading in dry skillet on medium heat, stirring constantly, for 5 to 7 minutes, until golden. Be careful; it burns easily. Beat egg whites until they hold stiff peaks. Combine coconut with condensed milk and vanilla, and fold in egg whites. Spoon by half-tablespoonfuls on cookie sheet and bake 10 to 12 minutes. Crunchy on the outside, moist and gooey on the inside.

Supper Under the Stars

The Atlanta Symphony Orchestra and sky-lighting pyrotechnics at Chastain Park make up one of Atlanta's more spectacular Independence Day celebrations. A program filled with Sousa marches and other patriotic favorites booms from the stage with bosom-swelling pride and a great sense of fun. The audience invariably gets in on the act, donning stars and stripes on their shorts and t-shirts, waving flags, and singing along. But then, Chastain is that kind of place.

I wrote about a house near Chastain Park in *Atlanta at Home*. And looking back, I notice that before I say a word about the house, I ramble on about the concerts at Chastain Park—about how they're one of the best things about summer in Atlanta. From classical to country to rock, the sounds of music emanate from the amphitheater nestled in a wooded, northwest Atlanta neighborhood replete with city golf course and riding stables. During performances, audiences as diverse as the music itself munch picnic suppers and sip wine. Tables and trays are set with everything from silver candelabra and crudités to paper plates and buckets of chicken. From late spring to early fall, the shows go on rain or shine, as usually do the encores—in answer to the flickering entreaty of the audience holding aloft hundreds of matches and candles, to light the way for more music in the night, a lovely sight.

Naturally, al fresco listening lends to al fresco dining, the only stipulation being that the dining not be so involved as to interfere with the socializing at first and the concert at last. Jane Long, of the well-known and well-loved "Easy Way Out" gourmet shop in Buckhead, knows just what to do: something prepared in advance and easily transported, and in not too many pieces—a simple, one- or two-dish meal and a little something sweet at the finish. This adaptation of Jane's Salmon Pasta Salad Niçoise is delectable and has enough of a little of everything to make it not only satisfying, but special—and pretty, too. The lemon tarts and ginger snaps are perfect with it.

And there you have it, a supper you can sing to.

Menu

**Summer Tomato Soup With Fresh Herbs and
Toasted French Bread**

Salmon Pasta Salad Niçoise

Lemon Tarts and Ginger Snaps

SERVES 4 TO 6

This is such a lovely menu for its making the most of fresh summer flavors. Everything can be made ahead. If you want to streamline, you can certainly omit the soup. If you still want to have a little appetizer, chop up a few tomatoes, add olive oil, fresh basil, garlic, and salt and pepper, and spoon it onto the toast in the recipe. The lemon tarts and ginger snaps go together wonderfully, and they of course don't have to be homemade, but they sure are good.

Summer Tomato Soup With Fresh Herbs And Toasted French Bread

It doesn't get any better, or easier, than this. Just for fun, we also tested this with two 28-ounce cans of plum tomatoes, and the results were surprisingly good.

6 to 8 best, ripe tomatoes,
   about 1½ pounds
1 tablespoon tomato paste
   (add only if fresh tomatoes lack flavor)
Salt and freshly ground pepper
1 tablespoon balsamic vinegar
1 teaspoon brown sugar
½ teaspoon coffee
   (left over from the morning or
   made from instant—
   a touch of coffee enhances the
   tomato flavor—go figure,
   but it does)

¾ tablespoon fresh, chopped tarragon,
   plus 4 sprigs of herb for garnish
   (or 1 whole tablespoon cilantro,
   basil, marjoram or dill—whatever
   you have on hand that is fresh;
   I just happen to like the
   tarragon with this menu
¾ heaping cup plain yogurt (or if
   you're trying to gain weight, ½ cup)
   heavy cream plus ¼ cup sour cream)
4 to 6 slices French or Italian
   peasant bread
1 tablespoon olive oil

Cut tomatoes in quarters and drop in food processor, no more than 4 tomatoes at a time. Process in short pulses to obtain a chunky puree. Place in bowl and add 1½ teaspoons of salt and 1 teaspoon pepper. Stir in remaining ingredients, reserving about ⅓ cup of yogurt. Cover and chill. To serve, ladle soup into bowls or cups and give each a dollop of yogurt (or sour cream) and a sprig of fresh herb. For the toast, slice bread ½ inch or slightly thicker, and brush both sides very lightly with olive oil. Toast on both sides until golden, but not brown.

Salmon Pasta Salad Niçoise

12 ounces salmon filet, poached
4 to 8 new potatoes,
   left whole, halved,
   or quartered, depending on size
¼ pound haricots vert
   (or green beans, cut in half)
8 ounces pasta—bowtie,
   rotelle, large shell, or penne
6 to 8 cherry tomatoes, cut in half
   (if you are serving the tomato soup,
   omit the tomatoes here)

1 small red onion, thinly sliced
⅓ cup black or Niçoise olives
2 tablespoons capers
2 tablespoons chopped fresh parsley
¼ cup Dijon mustard
1 tablespoon lemon juice
2 tablespoons white wine vinegar
1 garlic clove, crushed
½ cup olive oil
Salt and freshly ground pepper

Prepare all ingredients and have them sitting in one place. There is so much stuff in this you might easily forget something. If salmon is not already cooked, poach it in gently simmering (just below a boil) water, a little white wine, lemon slices and bay leaf, for 10 to 12 minutes, or until cooked through. Boil potatoes 15 to 20 minutes until tender. Blanch green beans in boiling water 3 to 4 minutes. Cook pasta al dente.

In large bowl, combine mustard, lemon juice and garlic, then whisk in olive oil in a thin stream. Add all other ingredients and season to taste. Toss with salad several hours ahead to allow flavors to meld.

Lemon Tarts

In trying to come up with the ideal, and easiest, recipe for this all-time favorite dessert, I think I made somewhere between 100 and 487,000 lemon tarts. And these are the best. Now, after hearing that, if you still have the heart to buy prepared lemon curd to plop into ready-made tart shells, well, I am the first to understand—but making them really is a breeze, I promise. Make the filling a day before, so it has a chance to chill and firm. This will make 1 large tart or 8 to 12 individual tarts, depending on size of tart shells. Use the leftover filling to spread on toast.

2 eggs plus 1 egg yolk
½ cup sugar
4 tablespoons butter,
    cut up in pieces
Juice and grated rind of
    1 large lemon, or 2 small

Pastry for one pie crust
1 9 or 10-inch tart pan
    with removable bottom or
    individual tart shells

In the top part of a double boiler, or in a heavy saucepan away from the heat, beat eggs and sugar together until fluffy and very pale yellow in color. Place over simmering water on medium low heat and add butter, juice and rind. Use a rubber spatula to scrape bottom and stir constantly until the mixture is very thick, 10 to 15 minutes. Remove from heat. To speed the chilling process, you may place the bowl in a larger bowl or sink of ice water and continue to stir it. Or set aside and cool, then cover and chill until ready to use. Will last several weeks in fridge.

Open air concerts at Chastain Park are a highlight of Atlanta's warm-weather months.

To make tart shells, roll out the pastry on a floured board, as called for on package or your recipe's directions. (I use the ready-made, refrigerated crusts that come folded up in plastic wrap, not in the pie tin.) If making a single large tart, press into tart pan with removable sides or into individual tart shells. Remember that with the small tarts, the crust-to filling ratio is greater, so you want the crust as thin as possible. Try to roll it out to between $1/8$ and $1/16$ of an inch. Cut rounds with a cookie cutter and fit them into the tart shells. Bake 9 to 12 minutes at 425°, until lightly golden.

Fill tart shells with lemon mixture up to 2 hours in advance—any more than that and the filling will make the crust soggy.

Ginger Snaps

Laced with tiny pieces of fresh and crystallized ginger, these are scrumptuous. Careful not to overbake them.

¾ cup dark brown sugar, firmly
   packed

½ cup canola oil

¼ cup molasses

1 egg

2 cups flour

2 teaspoons ground ginger

½ teaspoon salt

2 tablespoons baking soda

½ cup finely chopped crystallized ginger

1 ½ tablespoons finely chopped fresh
   ginger

In large bowl, combine sugar and oil, then add molasses and egg, beating well. Sift together flour, ginger, salt and baking soda, and add to bowl, followed by chopped ginger. Cover with plastic wrap and chill at least 2 hours. To bake, heat oven to 300°. Spray cookie sheet with nonstick spray, or lightly grease. Spoon out dough by the scant teaspoon, roll into ½ inch balls and place on a cookie sheet—cookies will flatten during baking. Bake for 10 minutes and cool on a rack.

Lunch With Soul

*T*t is difficult to define why or when it is that a kitchen and its cooking cross the line from "eating establishment" to "institution," but Burton's Grill is one that's done it. Begun off Buford Highway in 1930 and moved to Inman Park in 1961, this shrine to soul food has come to symbolize what is best about the old times and hopeful about the new. On the corner of Edgewood Avenue and Hurt Street, across from the MARTA station in an old brick building that still has a screen door, there is daily served old-fashioned Southern food, sweet tea, and Coca-Colas in the bottle.

On any given day you'll find construction workers, state troopers and neighborhood activists alongside big-time bankers, lawyers and politicians, all sharing some of the town's best fried chicken, and sometimes sharing a table. For years, in his two-and-a-half-foot-tall chef's hat, founder and proprietor Deacon Burton—he was also a deacon at Free for All Baptist Church in Decatur—would sit in a chair by the door, welcoming his many regulars. When he spied a newcomer, he'd ring a bell to get his patrons' attention. "This is Mr. so-and-so," the Deacon would holler, "All the way from Frankfurt, Germany! He's never had Deacon Burton's fried chicken before!"

Lyndell "Deacon" Burton's death in 1993 was front-page news in *The Atlanta Constitution*: "Atlanta loses a part of its soul with the death of Deacon Burton," mourned the headline. Writer Jack Warner called the grill "one of the city's most important culinary landmarks," and longtime customer Kevin Propst called it "probably the most culturally diverse place you can eat in the city." And from Congressman John Lewis, "I will deeply miss him."

On Christmas Eve night, 1924, young Lyndell ran away from his home in Watkinsville to seek his fortune in the city. By Christmas Day he had a job at a Greek restaurant downtown, washing dishes. Six years later, with $4,000 and a place on Plaster Avenue, Burton opened his eponymous grill at 5 in the morning and left in time to make the 7 a.m. shift at the old Henry Grady Hotel restaurant, leaving his wife Alice to run the grill. Burton would then return in the afternoon to cook and serve at his grill until midnight. Eventually, he moved the grill to Inman Park and left his outside day-job, but he took training to repair radios and TVs, and became a partner in a tour bus company, keeping the grill going all the while. He was profiled in *Life* magazine and invited by the British Broadcasting Company to come to London to appear on a cooking show. But the Deacon said he had too many customers and not enough help, and he just couldn't afford to close up that long.

From a center of civil rights activism to what has been called "a Mecca" for black businesses, Atlanta in 1959 adopted the slogan, "A city too busy to hate." Burton's Grill has stood for the truth in that statement, and for the optimism and good will it fosters. But then, judging from the grill during lunchtime, everyone is too busy eating or cooking to be worrying with anything else.

The traditional menu at Burton's Grill—fried chicken, catfish, cornbread, collards, yeast rolls and peach cobbler—is not an act I am even going to try to follow (although elsewhere in this book you'll find recipes for a few of these Southern favorites). What I've created is not to copy but to pay homage to a time-honored culinary tradition—with a contemporary sensibility—and offered in the same soulful spirit. It would make a good Sunday dinner. Amen, enjoy.

*M*ENU

Cold Sweet Potato Soup

Fried Chicken (from take-out)

Tangy Corn and Tomato Salad

Sugar Snap Peas

Homemade Biscuits (made in somebody else's home)

Banana Cream Puddin' and Pie

SERVES 8 TO 10

U.S. Representative John Lewis (right) enjoys lunch with constituents. When Deacon Burton (left) was alive, the congressman would have him up to Washington to cook for fundraising dinners.

I don't know why, but I'm just not ever going to fry a chicken. I sure am going to serve it every once in a (great) while, however, and when I do, I get it from a place that knows what it's doing, like Burton's Grill, or some other great fried chicken place. (By the way, I wouldn't exactly put Hardee's in the category of "great fried chicken places," but I happen to think they have great fried chicken. Great biscuits, too, and pretty good cole slaw. I realize all that could change, and it most certainly varies from place to place. But give it a try. It's convenient and the price is right.) The fried chicken would also work well with the "Happy Birthday" menu on page 126 or the "Juneteenth" menu (minus the meat dish) on page 50.

Cold Sweet Potato Soup

No, it isn't too sweet.

3 large sweet potatoes, not peeled
3 cups chicken or vegetable stock
4 leeks, white part only, chopped,
   (or 2 onions, chopped)
1/2 teaspoon ground ginger

1/2 teaspoon cinnamon
1/2 teaspoon nutmeg
1/4 teaspoon mace
2 (12-ounce) cans evaporated skim milk
2 tablespoons maple syrup

Pierce sweet potatoes with a fork, and bake, whole, in microwave (6 to 10 minutes), or oven (350° for 1 to 1½ hours), until soft. Split and scoop flesh into food processor. While baking, pour about ⅓ cup of broth into pot and add chopped leeks or onions and spices, and cook until soft. Put into food processor with sweet potatoes and another cup of broth, and puree. Pour back into pan and whisk in remaining broth, milk and maple syrup. Chill.

Fried Chicken and Biscuits

1 telephone	1 person to drive car
1 car	

Call chicken place and drive to pick up chicken and biscuits. If you want to serve chicken warm, pick it up as close to serving time as possible. Put on cookie sheet or platter and keep warm in oven. Don't wrap or cover because moisture will form and the chicken will get soggy. It's also just as good at room temperature or cold. Well, maybe not *quite* as good . . . To warm biscuits, wrap in foil and place in oven with chicken.

Tangy Corn and Tomato Salad

This is excellent and best made a few hours in advance, but take care: if you're making it more than a few hours ahead, save the tomatoes and cucumbers to add just before serving; otherwise their moisture will leak into the salad and dilute the flavors of the dressing—yuk.

2 medium tomatoes	4 tablespoons mayonnaise
1 medium cucumber, peeled	(low fat OK, but not nonfat)
1 green bell pepper	½ teaspoon dry mustard
1 small jalapeño pepper	2 tablespoons vinegar
1 medium purple onion, finely chopped	(herbed or pepper flavored OK)
3 cups canned shoepeg corn, drained	1 teaspoon celery seed
(or equivalent fresh or frozen)	Pinch of sugar
½ cup sour cream	Salt and freshly ground pepper
	Bibb lettuce, if desired for serving

Seed and chop first four ingredients. Sprinkle the tomatoes and cucumbers with salt, let sit for 15 to 30 minutes, rinse and pat dry. Combine with the rest and refrigerate. You may need to adjust the seasoning. Serve in Bibb lettuce leaves or as is.

Sugar Snap Peas

2 pounds sugar snap peas

2 tablespoons butter, melted

2 teaspooons fresh lemon juice

Salt

Working the fryers at Burton's grill, an Atlanta institution since 1930.

Bring large pot of water to boil and cook peas 2-4 minutes, until crisp-tender. Drain and run under cold water or immerse in iced water to stop cooking. Toss with melted butter and lemon juice, and season to taste.

Banana Cream Puddin' and Pie

This might also be called "Mile-High Banana and Coconut Cream Puddin' and Pie," but it's too long. My own concoction, and heavenly, if I do say so myself. A cookie recipe inspired the crust, and it is rich and good enough to be eaten by itself. The banana chips you can find in health food stores and in the bulk containers at grocery stores. You also find them in small packages, sometimes displayed with "trail mix" and such. A meringue topping, instead of the whipped cream, will work for this as well. Just look up a recipe for lemon meringue pie and make the meringue part, then bake as the recipe says.

1 ½ cups toasted coconut, divided into ½ cup, ¾ cup, and ¼ cup
½ cup (1 stick) butter
1 (12-ounce) box vanilla wafers
½ cup sweetened banana chips
½ cup macadamia nuts (optional)
3 tablespoons flour, divided
¼ teaspoon cinnamon

¾ cup sugar plus 2 tablespoons sugar
3 eggs plus 1 yolk
3 ½ cups milk
3 teaspoons vanilla, divided into 2 and 1
¼ teaspoon freshly grated nutmeg
4–5 bananas
1 ½ cups heavy whipping cream

To Toast Coconut
Place in large nonstick skillet over medium heat and "toast," shaking and stirring pan for 5 to 7 minutes. Watch it like a hawk. It will look like it isn't cooking at all, then all of a sudden it starts turning brown. It burns easily. Aim for a golden brown color.

Crust

Heat oven to 350°. In bowl of food processor, combine ½ cup of the coconut, the butter, 1½ cups vanilla wafers, the bananas, nuts, 2 tablespoons flour and cinnamon and process to coarse crumb consistency. Or mash by hand with a pastry mixer. Press dough into bottom and sides of 10-inch, deep-dish pie plate. Bake 7 minutes until lightly browned.

Filling

In heavy saucepan over medium heat, combine ¾ cup sugar and 1 tablespoon flour, and beat in eggs one at a time. Slowly stir in the milk, and continue stirring until mixture thickens and coats the back of the spoon, about 7 minutes. Do not boil. Remove from heat and stir in ¾ cup coconut, 1 teaspoon vanilla, and freshly grated nutmeg. Chill.

To assemble, place one layer of sliced bananas on bottom of pie crust, and a layer of vanilla wafers on top of that. Cover with half the custard. Repeat the layers once more, ending with custard. To serve, whip the cream with 2 tablespoons sugar and 1 teaspoon vanilla and mound atop the pie in swirls and peaks. Sprinkle with the remaining toasted coconut.

A Canopied Feast

*A*tlantan Brooks Garcia knows gardens and garden design. And Atlanta knows he knows, as evidenced by Brooks's inspired work growing and blooming all over town, not the least of which are a flourishing cottage garden in an apartment courtyard on East Paces Ferry Road, the wonderland he created behind his mother's brick ranch house near Chastain Park, and the rather grand European-style garden he installed at the corner of Habersham and Valley roads in Buckhead, to cite a few.

Brooks also knows fun parties. A former protégé of preeminent garden (and party) designer Ryan Gainey, Brooks's natural inclinations toward creative entertaining were further cultivated during his days with Ryan, whom, Brooks graciously acknowledges, "was always an inspiration." And now Brooks shines in his own right, in his own business, Fine Gardens. So why shouldn't he celebrate? A birthday is as good a time as any. "It's really more of a party for my friends than for myself," he demurs. "I love the idea of creating a memorable moment with and for my friends—because memory is possession."

Such poetry could only come from a romantic soul, both enhanced and amused, says he, "by all the romantic things that touch my life." In gardens, flowers, art, and even movies, are the seeds of his ideas. It was a Moroccan-themed party Brooks helped Ryan with in Long Island one summer that Brooks later adapted for his own. In Atlanta, in his mother's gorgeous garden, Brooks fashioned a tented, outdoor dining room draped in seventy-five yards of dyed orange muslin. Beneath it he set a low octagonal table he'd had made; surrounded it with fat, comfy pillows; and hung wondrous, handmade lanterns flickering light over a veritable sultan's feast. A favorite painting by John Singer Sargent of a young girl lighting paper lanterns in a garden gave Brooks the idea for the lanterns, which he invited guests to make and bring. "That gets people involved and excited about what's to come," says the host, who laced the tree-branches with string, from which the varyingly lovely, wacky, funny and bizarre, but absolutely original, lanterns were suspended. The table was spread with a bright Moroccan print and be-flowered with roses and amaranths in vivid reds and oranges—dazzling as a desert sunset.

The feast began with fresh melons, figs, olives, apricots, cashews and dates—all in pretty bowls set around the table. It was a grazing affair, with courses served at a leisurely pace, and nibbling in between. "That allows everyone to visit," says Brooks—as does cooking the kabobs at a little grill right by the table. The key was to minimize time away from the company, who, on this night not only pitched in, but might gladly have swum the Mediterranean or trekked the Sahara to partake of this meal and possess the memory.

This menu combines some of Brooks's dishes and some of my own. The result is perhaps more broadly Mediterranean than specifically Moroccan, but there is no compromising on taste. This is an occasion—camp it up, wear costumes, decorate, play exotic music, and let it last all night, because the food surely will.

*M*ENU

Turkish Melons, Bunches of Grapes, Roasted Almonds and Cashews, Stuffed Grape Leaves, Savory Pita Strips, Hummus, Roasted Garlic, Variety of Olives and Herbs

Lamb, Beef and Chicken Kabobs

Couscous With Vegetables

Carrots With Lemon and Mint

Figs Stuffed With Camembert, Dates Stuffed With Cream Cheese and Ginger, Fragrant Marinated Oranges

SERVES 8 TO 12

So I got a little carried away. Or Brooks did. Look, this is a lot of food. I don't really expect you to do all this unless you are going all out. Pick and choose what you like and have time for. Because of the manner of serving and ease of preparation of some of the dishes, this is a great menu for inviting last-minute guests—it isn't the loaves and fishes, but it does seem to go on forever. As for the nibbles on the table to begin, use purchased melons, grapes, nuts, stuffed grape leaves (called Dolmades), and pita bread. You may also used prepared hummus, but a recipe is included here.

Savory Pita Strips

This is an ancient entry in my "Kitchen Secrets" started for me long ago—and continually updated—by my mother, who wrote, "I adore them and have never had anything similar. You can do them ahead and keep tightly tinned."

3 to 4 pieces pita bread   Parmesan cheese
Butter, softened   Dried dill
Onion Salt

Heat oven to 325°. Split each piece of pita into its two halves, and lightly butter the inside of each half. Cut into strips about 1 inch wide by 2 inches long. Sprinkle lightly with onion salt, then Parmesan cheese. Sprinkle dill on top. Bake on cookie sheet for 10 to 15 minutes, until barely browned. Watch closely. Each pita half makes about 12 small strips, so 3 pieces of pita bread will make 6 dozen strips. (Of course this may vary depending on the size of the bread.)

Hummus

This is wonderful with toasted pita bread, grilled or roasted vegetables, and as an accompaniment to grilled meats.

1 can (15 ounces) chickpeas,
   rinsed and drained
$1/4$ cup fresh lemon juice
$1/4$ cup tahini (sesame paste)
$1/4$ cup plain yogurt (nonfat OK)
2 tablespoons minced fresh cilantro
   (or parsley)

1 garlic clove, minced
$1/2$ teaspoon ground cumin
1 teaspoon paprika
$1/4$ teaspoon salt (or to taste)

Combine all ingredients in food processor or blender and blend until smooth.

Roasted Garlic

You may use regular garlic or the larger, milder tasting elephant garlic. In any case, choose bulbs which are plump, firm and have some weight to them. Avoid light and flaky heads (dried out) and those with sprouts (old and bitter). Roasted garlic may be used for a number of yummy things—squeezed into mashed potatoes, for example, or in any pasta or pizza, or grilled meat. You might also try mixing it with ricotta cheese and black pepper as a dip for vegetables.

3 large heads of garlic
1 tablespoon olive oil

Toasted pita bread

Heat oven to 425°. Wrap each whole, unpeeled head in foil and roast 20 to 25 minutes, until soft. Let cool, then cut a very thin slice off the bottom of each head. To serve, pour the olive oil into the center of a small serving plate and swirl it around to cover, then place garlic on plate. To eat, break cloves apart and squeeze the garlic out of the bottom of each one. Good with toasted pita or toasted thin slices of French bread.

Lamb, Beef and Chicken Kabobs

This marinade works well with all three of these meats, and it's kind of fun to have a variety. But by all means use any combination you like, and be sure to have your butcher do the chopping. The aroma while cooking is intoxicating, and the flavor is all it promises to be. Allow several hours for meat to marinate.

1 pound each lamb, beef and chicken breast, cut into 3/4-inch chunks
1 large onion, finely chopped
1/3 cup olive oil
1 tablespoon lemon juice
1/3 cup chopped fresh cilantro
1/2 cup chopped fresh parsley

4 to 6 cloves garlic, crushed
1 teaspoon salt
1 teaspoon cumin
1/2 teaspoon red pepper
1/4 teaspoon red pepper flakes
Small wooden skewers, soaked in water for 20 minutes

Thread each kind of meat on its own skewers, as their cooking times vary. Combine remaining ingredients (You can do it all in the food processor). Spoon over the meats and refrigerate for at least 3 or 4 hours, stirring occasionally.

Prepare grill or preheat oven to 400°. Thread 4 or 5 pieces onto skewers and grill or roast, turning to cook evenly. The cooking times will vary according to your preference and the cuts of meat you choose. The lamb and beef should take 15 to 20 minutes; the chicken about 10 minutes, so put it on last. Serve on a bed of Couscous With Vegetables.

Couscous With Vegetables

Don't be put off by the length of this recipe. It is a rather exotic dish but made from readily available ingredients. Preparation is simple—just have everything measured and ready in advance, and you're all but finished. Tip: Chop the onion and pepper in the food processor—it doesn't matter what they look like; the other vegetables will make it pretty enough. Also, if you are not serving this with a side dish of carrots, add 2 chopped carrots and sauté with the onion. You may also add turnips or potatoes.

3 ½ cups chicken or beef broth, plus
   1 more cup (to reserve
   for vegetables)
¼ cup chopped fresh parsley
1 teaspoon dried thyme
1 teaspoon curry powder
2 cups quick-cooking couscous,
   about 14 ounces
1 medium onion, chopped
2 cloves garlic, minced
2 medium zucchini, chopped
1 medium turnip,
   peeled and chopped
1 can (15 ounces) white beans
   (or chick peas), rinsed and drained
1 cup frozen lima beans, thawed
6 sundried tomatoes,
   soaked in hot water
   for 20 minutes and sliced

2 fresh tomatoes, chopped,
   or 1 can (20 ounces) plum tomatoes,
   drained and chopped
3 tablespoons chopped fresh chives
   or scallions
¼ cup chopped dried apricots
   (or golden raisins)
1 cup frozen green peas, thawed

Dressing
1 teaspoon paprika
½ teaspoon coriander
½ teaspoon saffron threads
2 tablespoons fresh lemon juice
2 tablespoons olive oil
2 cloves garlic, crushed
Pinch of cayenne or red pepper

Place 3 ½ cups broth in large pot with a lid. Add parsley, thyme and curry.

In another large skillet or pot pour ¼ cup of the remaining broth and sauté onion and garlic on medium-high heat until soft. Add the last ¾ cup of stock, vegetables, apricots, paprika and saffron, and lower heat to medium. Cover and cook for another 10 minutes, removing cover to stir occasionally, then remove from heat. You can make ahead to this point. When ready to serve, stir peas into vegetables and make the couscous as follows: Bring broth, herb and spice mixture to boil and stir in couscous. Cover and remove from heat. Let stand, covered tightly, for 10 minutes.

Meantime, combine dressing ingredients in small jar or separate bowl. When couscous is ready, pour mixture over and fluff with a fork. Serve couscous on a warm platter with the vegetables mounded in the center.

Left: Guests were instructed to make and bring their own lanterns, which yielded whimsical, luminous results. Right: The rich and vibrant colors of the tabletop complement the bold earthiness of the food.

Carrots With Lemon and Mint

Even people who do not like carrots love these. Their touch of sweetness makes them especially good with spicy foods and grilled meats.

1 1/2 to 2 pounds miniature carrots (or regular carrots, sliced)	2 teaspoons cornstarch
1 teaspoon salt	3 tablespoons butter
2 teaspoons sugar	Grated peel and juice of 1 lemon
	1/4 cup chopped fresh mint

You will want to save 2/3 cup of the carrot-cooking liquid, so don't forget. And be sure your mint is dry before chopping, or it will glob together.

Now, bring about 3 cups water to boil. Add carrots and 2 teaspoons salt, and cook 5 or 6 minutes, until crisp-tender. You'll hate yourself if you overcook them. Taste-test for doneness—the baby carrots take longer than the sliced or chopped ones. Drain and save 2/3 cup of the liquid.

In small separate bowl, combine sugar and cornstarch.

In large saucepan, melt butter and stir in (in order) cornstarch mixture, reserved cooking liquid, and lemon peel and juice. Cook over medium heat until a little bit thickened, 5 to 7 minutes. Add almost all of the mint, reserving a little to sprinkle on just before serving.

If making ahead, refrigerate. To serve, gently reheat and sprinkle with remaining fresh mint.

Figs Stuffed With Camembert

A heavenly combination of flavors best brought out at room temperature.

$^1/_4$ pound (4 ounces) Camembert (or Brie) cheese	16 dried figs (about $^1/_2$ pound)
	$^1/_4$ cup port wine

Trim rind from cheese and cut into 16 pieces, or as many pieces as you have figs, and place in a small bowl. Pour port over and marinate at least 2 hours. When ready to assemble, pour off port and reserve. Cut a slit in the top of each fig, just to the side of the stem end, and work a little space inside it with your finger. Stuff with the cheese. Place in shallow bowl and pour reserved port over.

Dates Stuffed With Cream Cheese and Ginger

$^1/_4$ pound (4 ounces) cream cheese, softened	1 teaspoon grated lemon peel
1 heaping tablespoon chopped, crystallized ginger	1 teaspoon fresh lemon juice
	$^1/_2$ pound dried, pitted dates (15 to 25, depending on size)

Blend together first three ingredients and stuff into dates. They will be slightly messy, as some of the cheese will stick out of the dates. Lick your fingers and enjoy.

Fragrant Marinated Oranges

So light and refreshing after a big meal, with just the right touch of sweetness. What gives this its distinctive flavor is the relatively obscure ingredient of orange flower water. It is supposedly available in specialty food stores, but I finally tracked it down in a liquor store, with the liqueurs. If, alas, you cannot find it, the Variation is wonderful, but omit dates elsewhere in the menu.

6 to 8 navel oranges, peeled of
   rind and all white pith
1 tablespoon orange flower water
$1/3$ cup orange juice

$1/3$ cup honey
Scant $1/3$ cup chopped, unsalted
   pistachios (or toasted pine nuts)

Cut peeled oranges into $1/3$-inch thick slices and place in shallow bowl. Combine juice, honey and orange flower water and pour over top. Cover and chill at least an hour, but no more than 4 hours. Serve sprinkled with chopped pistachios or toasted pine nuts.

Variation With Rum, Dates and Pine Nuts
To oranges (as above) add $1/3$ cup orange juice, $1/3$ cup dark rum and $1/3$ cup minced dates. Cover and chill for at least an hour. When serving, sprinkle with toasted pine nuts.

90

The Garden of Eden Ball

*T*he Atlanta Botanical Garden is without doubt one of the city's most precious treasures. Five minutes from downtown, on thirty acres in Piedmont Park, what began in 1977 as an old office trailer surrounded by scraggly overgrowth is today a superlative and scrupulously maintained public garden, one of the finest in the country. The gleaming glass and steel Fuqua Conservatory is as stunning architecturally as it is important botanically, housing rare, endangered and exotic species. The grounds comprise a rose garden, Japanese garden, ornamental grasses and herbs, vegetables, a carnivorous plant bog, a naturalized woodland area, and a beautifully manicured "Great Lawn." There is also a forest of hardwoods, called the Storza Woods, which is a rare, if not sacred, resource in an urban setting. And in early spring, the Southeastern Flower Show, with its glorious array of landscape designs, masterful arrangements and myriad exhibits, is held to benefit the Garden and attracts tens of thousands of visitors every year.

Another event in the Garden's behalf may be smaller in scale but is grand in execution. As to significance, it is the largest single fundraiser of the year. And for the handful of Atlantans who attend, it is a lovely rite of autumn. The Garden of Eden Ball began in 1980 and is continually unsurpassed for elaborateness, with themes visiting ancient Babylon, the opulent Orient, and colonial East Africa, to name a few. So it was somewhat of a departure when ball chairman Mary Bray wanted not so much to downscale but to relax things somewhat. (She even lobbied valiantly for abandoning the black ties just this once, but was swiftly assured of no such thing.) Nonetheless, Mary's "Fête de Provence" was carried off with *élan*, owing in part to the guidance of Ryan Gainey—*tour de force* floral designer and Francophile, and the last word on just-right rustic elegance.

Tables were draped with Souleiado fabrics in the sun-drenched palettes of the Impressionists, set upon alternately by bouquets of sunflowers, topiaries of herbs, and mounds of lavender amid artichokes, aubergines, and ropes of garlic—all artfully arranged around wrought iron candelabra. An open-air effect was lent by the clear tent, which was hell on the committee decorating in the steaming September sun, but something else at night, when the lights were dimmed and . . . *boom!* Fireworks sprayed and danced across the sky, among the stars, above the tent. Guests gasped with delight, and then danced all night.

The menu of Provençal foods prepared by the Ritz-Carlton Atlanta was delightful as well, with lamb, *haricots verts*, *pommes de terre*, and *tartes au citron*. My menu here is likewise inspired, but I've varied it a bit in part to be original and in part to keep balance with the book's other menus. *Bon Appétit.*

ENU

Field Greens With Smoked Salmon and Chèvre with Cream Cheese Dressing and Toast Points

Herb Stuffed Roast Lamb With Bernaise

Rosemary and Thyme Potatoes

Haricots Verts With Garlic and Mint

Orange Crème Caramel

Delicate Butter Almond Cookies

SERVES 8

Elizabeth James, of Atlanta's Company Co. caterers, is well known and revered for her always very good food. She is a consistent crowd-pleaser with an excellent sense not only of what people will like, but of what food best fits the occasion. Her menu here is neither elaborate nor difficult, and it can mostly be prepared in advance. The Crème Caramel was developed with Candy Sheehan, and I added the cookies for a light crunch—satisfying after this wonderful meal of Elizabeth's.

To simplify: Of course, you can always skip the first course. Do, instead, a little smoked salmon with cream cheese and/or crème fraiche, capers, lemon and toast points (or similar) for hors d'oeuvres. Don't skimp on the lamb or potatoes; they deserve all they ask. But you can marinate the blanched green beans with good quality prepared vinaigrette, tossing in a few crushed mint leaves (so good with the lamb) and toasted walnuts. For dessert, pass a little plate of gourmet cookies and chocolates. It's a nice touch, and feels pampering, somehow.

Field Greens With Smoked Salmon and Chèvre

Use any combination that's fresh and available—red and curly leaf lettuces, Romaine, endive, arugula, radicchio, watercress.

8 ounces smoked salmon,   8 ounces chèvre (goat cheese)
   in paper-thin slices

Cream Cheese Dressing

Reduced fat cream cheese and sour cream work fine for this, but don't say I said so. Elizabeth is a purist. Up to you.

8 ounces cream cheese, softened   1 tablespoon lemon juice
2 tablespoons sour cream   2 tablespoons chopped fresh dill
1 tablespoon prepared horseradish,   1/4 cup capers, reserving
   drained (more or less to taste)   at least 1–2 tablespoons of the juice

Blend cream cheese and sour cream (can do in food processor). Add horseradish, lemon and caper juices, then stir in dill and capers. Thickness will depend upon grades of cream cheese and sour cream used. If too thick, thin with a little more lemon or caper juice.

Toast Points

(Yummy, but optional)

8 thin slices bread   Jane's Krazy Mixed-Up Salt®
Butter

Trim edges from bread, brush with melted butter and sprinkle with Jane's Salt. Bake at 350° 5 to 10 minutes until crisp.

TO ASSEMBLE

Arrange lettuce on plates and pour small amount of dressing over. Top with the salmon and crumbled goat cheese. Serve toast points on the side. Pass extra dressing.

Herb Stuffed Roast Lamb With Bernaise

This is excellent with Bernaise sauce, and Elizabeth's recipe is included here. I often do not sauté onions, garlic, mushrooms in butter; chicken stock, white wine or water do as well and do not add fat. Speaking of fat, make the Bernaise the very last thing you do before serving the main course. Also, a meat thermometer is very handy for this—and any—roasted meat dish.

Herb Stuffed Roast Lamb

1 leg of lamb, boned and butterflied
    (should be about 4 pounds
    without the bone)
2 (16-ounce) bags frozen spinach,
    thawed, drained and squeezed of
    all excess water.
1 medium onion, finely chopped
    (can use food processor)

5–6 cloves garlic, peeled and chopped
2–3 tablespoons butter for sautéing,
    or equivalent stock or wine
1 bag (8 ounces) Pepperidge Farm®
    Country Garden Herb Stuffing Mix
1 tablespoon fresh lemon juice
Sea salt (or other coarse salt)
    and freshly ground pepper

Sauté onion and garlic over low heat for just a few minutes. Add spinach and stuffing mix, lemon juice, salt and pepper. Stuff the lamb and tie with string (Ask your butcher to help if you need to). Then rub with one of the marinades. Preheat oven to 325°. Bake lamb for about 1½ hours, depending on quality and thickness of meat. Use meat thermometer. An internal temperature of 135° to 140° is rare; 150° is medium.

Lamb Marinade I

This is Elizabeth's. She swears by it, and so do our testers.

1–2 tablespoons olive oil   Harold's Seasoning*
Sea salt and freshly ground pepper

Rub salt, pepper and Harold's Seasoning (if available) over stuffed, tied lamb. Then rub over with a little olive oil, to help retain juices.

*Available at The New Yorker Deli, formerly Harold's, at 322 Pharr Road, in the Buckhead area of Atlanta, (404) 240-0260. If you live outside the city, they will send it to you by mail, and it is worth your trouble. It is nothing more than salt, pepper, garlic and onion but somehow there is magic in the proportions. You can also use an alternative marinade, such as the very good but slightly more involved one in the recipe below. If you cannot get the Harold's and don't want to fool with another marinade, then salt, pepper and olive oil will do just fine.

Lamb Marinade II

This is my own recipe, and very good.

2 cloves garlic, crushed   1 tablespoon dried rosemary
1 teaspoon each salt and pepper   ¼ cup olive oil
¼ teaspoon powdered ginger   2 tablespoons red wine vinegar
1 tablespoon dried marjoram   1 tablespoon orange marmealade, melted

Combine all ingredients and rub over outside of stuffed and tied lamb.

Bernaise Sauce

¼ cup dry white wine

¼ cup wine vinegar

¼ cup minced parsley,
   plus a little extra for garnish

1 green onion, finely chopped

1 teaspoon dried tarragon

½ teaspoon salt

¼ teaspoon pepper

3 egg yolks

1 cup (2 sticks) butter, melted

Combine wine, vinegar, parsley, green onion, tarragon, salt and pepper. Bring to a boil and reduce to 3 or 4 tablespoons. Strain, pressing on solids to get all the flavor.

Heat butter to bubbling, but watch that it doesn't brown. Put egg yolks in food processsor and process 20 seconds. With machine running, begin adding butter through feed tube drop by drop (so it doesn't cook the yolks); then add by teaspoons until it begins to thicken. Add remaining butter in thin stream, then stir in reduced wine mixture. Adjust seasonings and add fresh parsley to garnish. Makes 1½ cups.

Rosemary and Thyme Potatoes

16 or more new potatoes,
    left whole or cut in half,
    depending on size
2–3 tablespoons olive oil

Sea or kosher salt
2 tablespoons fresh rosemary
2 tablespoons fresh thyme

Heat oven to 350°. Toss potatoes with olive oil, salt and herbs. Spread potatoes on cookie sheet and bake about 1 hour, or until fork-tender. Shake pan occasionally to prevent sticking. Turn oven up to broil for the last 5 minutes or so, for crispy outsides.

Haricots Verts With Garlic and Mint

2 pounds French green beans
    (called *haricots verts*) if available;
    regular green beans otherwise
2 teaspoons salt
½ teaspoon baking powder

4 tablespoons (½ stick) of butter
2 cloves garlic, crushed
Small bunch of mint leaves,
    crushed (save 8 extra mint sprigs for
    dessert)

Prepare beans and bring large pot of water to boil. Add salt and baking powder. In sink, fill another container (big enough to hold beans) with iced water. Blanch beans in boiling water for about 1½ minutes, then plunge into iced water to stop cooking. Drain and set aside.

Melt butter and add garlic. Toss with green beans. Sprinkle with crushed mint just before serving.

The Garden of Eden Ball is held every autumn to benefit the Atlanta Botanical Garden. A "Fête de Provence," designed by Ryan Gainey, evoked the warm, rustic elegance of the south of France.

Orange Crème Caramel

A different version of this classic French favorite—lightly spiced with citrus essence. Developed with the help of talented Atlanta chef, Candy Sheehan.

⅓ cup plus ½ cup sugar	Grated rind of 1 orange
2 cups milk	1 teaspoon vanilla
4 eggs	⅛ teaspoon ground cloves

Have all ingredients measured and prepared at the start; this goes quickly once you begin it. Put a large baking pan (large enough to hold 10-inch pie plate or shallow casserole dish) in the oven and fill it one-fourth full with water. Heat oven to 350°. With electric mixer beat together the ⅓ cup of sugar and all other ingredients except remaining ½ cup sugar, skimming off foam when finished.

In small saucepan over high heat, add the remaining sugar and cook, stirring constantly until boiling and caramelized (golden colored). Pour in bottom of round 10-inch pie or casserole dish. Pour egg mixture on top. Bake for 1 hour, until set. Refrigerate several hours or overnight. When ready to serve, put the dish in a little hot water to melt and loosen the bottom slightly. Loosen sides with a knife and invert onto serving plate, letting the caramel run over it.

Delicate Almond Butter Cookies

These little delectables are similar to the French tuiles or "tiles," so called because they are draped over a rolling pin to cool and the resulting curved shape resembles that of the red roofing tiles typical in the south of France. You may do the same with this miniature version, or just let them be flat.

¼ cup sugar

4 tablespoons (½ stick)
  butter, softened

¼ cup flour

⅓ cup ground almonds

1 egg white

1 tablespoon milk

¼ teaspoon vanilla

⅛ teaspoon almond extract

⅓ cup sliced almonds

Grease a cookie sheet (or two) and heat oven to 325°.

Cream butter and sugar, then combine all ingredients except sliced almonds and drop by teaspoonfuls 2 inches apart on cookie sheet. They spread a lot. After 2 minutes, open oven door and sprinkle cookies with a few sliced almonds. Close door and bake about 3 minutes more. If you want to imitate the French *tuiles*, remove the hot cookies immediately and drape them over a rolling pin to cool. Otherwise cool for a minute on the cookie sheet before removing to a rack.

Humidity will wilt these. To re-crisp, place on a cookie sheet and warm at 250° for a minute or two.

An Autumn Picnic

*A*tlanta has been called a city of trees, and at the right time of year, trees are wonderful places under which to have picnics. In the Buckhead neighborhood of Atlanta, few harbingers of autumn are more glorious than the pair of ginkgo trees at the entrance to Peachtree Battle Avenue from Peachtree Road. Their dazzling gold foliage spread against a cerulean November sky is, literally, a traffic-stopper. Not to mention a photo opportunity. Mamas from all over dress up their babies and bring them here to loll about in the bright yellow leaves and giggle and laugh and have their pictures taken. And taken.

But these noble trees have a more serious purpose, too. As a memorial, the trees are towering, silent sentries guarding a stone marker erected in 1935, honoring the brave men who fought on this site in the Civil War. It is also, reads the marker, "a tribute to American valor, which they of the Blue and they of the Gray had as a common heritage, from the forefathers of 1776 to the pervading spirit thereof, which, in the days 1898 and the Great World Conflict of 1917–1918, perfected the reunion of the North and the South."

When Alisa Barry marshaled her culinary forces in Atlanta, the city didn't burn, but it sure sat up and took notice. Her training at culinary-cutting-edge restaurants in Los Angeles and her imaginative approach to everyday food consistently results in new takes on old favorites and stunning combinations of classic ingredients to create new classics of her own. The erstwhile "Bella Cucina," a hip, Italian-ish café and catering shop in the Buckhead Interiors Market, daily proffered such glories as grilled eggplant and roasted peppers with provolone on rosemary focaccia bread; egg salad with pesto aïoli on olive bread; specials like quail wrapped in prosciutto on greens with gorgonzola, walnuts and grilled portabello mushrooms; and her famous Death by Chocolate cookies. Today, her "Bella Cucina" packaged products grace the shelves of such chi-chi enclaves as Barney's and Bergdorf Goodman. And now, a bit of Bella Cucina—with recipes adapted for the regular-person cook—can grace your picnic basket as well.

**Lemon Sage Roasted Game Hens
With Cranberry Pear Walnut Chutney**

Green Bean Bundles

Onion, Fresh Thyme and Goat Cheese Pizzas

Fresh Pear and Ginger Tart

SERVES 4

This menu is a simplified version of Alisa's original, but the recipes are designed specifically to be made ahead and to be wonderful at room temperature—it is a picnic, after all. To simplify even further: Even though Alisa would fall on her own whisk before using storebought stuff, well, we just can't always be like Alisa. So, if you must (and let's face it, sometimes you must), buy already roasted chickens or chicken parts and let it go at that, or rub the outsides with a mixture of half lemon juice and half olive oil and a spoonful each of chopped thyme and sage. Wrap them in foil or plastic bags and refrigerate overnight. Use prepared chutney or skip it altogether. For the pizzas, you could put the goat cheese mixture on prepared pizza crusts and bake it 5 or 10 minutes, then off you go. The soft bread stick refrigerated dough will also substitute for the homemade. Shape into small rounds and brush with olive oil before topping with goat cheese mixture and baking according to package directions. The green bean bundles are easy. And if you skip the tart, take ginger snaps and fresh pears instead. By the way, a great recipe for homemade ginger snaps appears on page 70.

Roasted Cornish hens, green bean bundles, goat cheese pizzas, and a fresh pear tart capture the bounty and flavors of fall—prepared ahead and transported with ease. With Alisa, designer Smith Hanes created a charming and stylish picnic setting.

Lemon Sage Roasted Game Hens

If you cannot find fresh sage, rosemary is just as good.

4 Cornish game hens, cleaned,
   rinsed and dried

Salt and freshly ground pepper

2 lemons, cut in half

1 bunch fresh sage

8 cloves garlic

4 tablespoons olive oil

4 tablespoons chopped fresh garlic

Heat oven to 375°. Sprinkle inside of each hen with 1 teaspoon salt and 1/2 teaspoon pepper. Squeeze 1 half-lemon into each one and use the lemon itself to rub the juice around; then leave it inside the cavity, along with 2 sage sprigs and 2 garlic cloves. Tuck 2 large sage leaves under the breast skin of each hen. Mix the olive oil with chopped garlic, salt and pepper, and rub the outside of each hen. Then truss (tie legs together) with heavy string or raffia. Roast breast-side down for 30 minutes and

breast side up for another 20 to 30 minutes, or until juices run clear when poked with the tip of a sharp knife. Serve warm or at room temperature. Hens may be cut down middle of breast bone for smaller portions.

Cranberry Pear Walnut Chutney

1 pound fresh cranberries

1 ripe pear, peeled and
cut into 1/4-inch pieces

1 cup apple juice
(or 3/4 cup juice and
1/4 cup red wine or port)

1 cup sugar

1 teaspoon each allspice,
cloves and cinnamon

1/2 cup chopped, toasted walnuts

In heavy saucepan, combine all except walnuts and cook over medium heat until cranberries begin to burst, 20–30 minutes. Add walnuts.

Green Bean Bundles

1 large green stem of a leek,
or several green stems from
green onions

1 pound green beans,
or mix half green beans
and half yellow wax beans, if available

Into a large pot of boiling, salted water, dip the leek or green onion stems for about one minute. Remove and drape over the sink or somewhere to cool. Into same boiling water, blanch beans for about 5 minutes. Remove and drain, running cold water over them to stop the cooking. Better yet, plunge them into a bowl of iced water. Then, with a thin strip of blanched leek or green onion, tie up with a knot four little bundles of beans.

Onion, Fresh Thyme and Goat Cheese Pizzas

These are a tremendous hit. And the pizza dough can of course be used for a range of toppings.

Pizza Dough

Don't be intimidated. There is nothing hard or tricky about this. Allow about 3 hours, during most of which time the dough is rising and you can be doing something else. Just don't forget about it.

1/4 cup lukewarm water	1 tablespoon milk
2 teaspoons yeast	2 tablespoons olive oil
1/4 cup plus 1 3/4 cups all-purpose flour	1/2 teaspoon salt
1/2 cup lukewarm water	

Combine 1/4 cup lukewarm water, yeast and 1/4 cup flour. Let stand for 20 minutes, then add remaining ingredients. Mix thoroughly. On a floured board, knead for about 10 minutes until soft but still moist. (This moistness makes the crust crispy.) Place in a lightly oiled bowl, turning once to coat. Cover with a towel and put in warm place to rise for 2 hours, or until doubled in size. Punch it down and let it rise another 40 minutes. After the second rising, shape dough into 4 balls and let rest. While it rests, make the topping.

Pizza Topping

2 medium red onions, thinly sliced	8 ounces goat cheese
2 tablespoons olive oil	1/4 cup chopped fresh thyme,
1/4 cup water	and sprigs for garnish
2 tablespoons red wine vinegar	Olive oil for brushing pizza dough

Sauté onion in olive oil until soft. Add water and vinegar and cook until liquid is absorbed. Set aside to cool.

Heat oven to 400°. Roll out dough balls to 1/2 inch thick. Brush with olive oil. Divide onion mixture evenly and spread on each pizza. Crumble goat cheese over onion and sprinkle with thyme. Let rise 20 minutes. Bake 30–40 minutes until crisp. (If you have a pizza stone, use it. Otherwise use a lightly greased metal cookie sheet.)

Fresh Pear and Ginger Tart

This is my own recipe, different, but easy and delectable. I use a prepared, refrigerated crust and press it into a tart tin with fluted edges and removable bottom. If there is someone who doesn't like ginger, try substituting chocolate wafers for the ginger snaps.

1 pie or tart shell,
   baked 10-12 minutes at 350°,
   but with edges shielded by foil
1/2 cup ginger snap crumbs
4 ripe pears

1 tablespoon sugar
1/4 teaspoon ground ginger
1/4 teaspoon cinnamon
1/4 cup honey
1 tablespoon lemon juice

Preheat oven to 375°. Sprinkle ginger snap crumbs on bottom of baked tart shell. Peel and slice pears lengthwise, and arrange atop ginger snap crumbs. Combine sugar and spices and sprinkle onto pears. Bake 25–30 minutes. Warm honey and lemon juice together, and brush onto tart while still warm.

A Night for the Opera

A stunning autumn table may be adorned exclusively with the fruits and flora of the season. Maple leaves are raked into a centerpiece of softly layered red and gold, with votives in clay pots and condiments in autumn-hued crockery. A wrought-iron epergne is entwined in the fading greens of grapes and vines, topped by a small, carved bird perched on a pumpkin in a nest of leaves. Leaves as place-mats are in pretty contrast to pale ocher damask linens, and assorted pottery plates are amicable companions to hand-blown goblets. The feeling is almost that of an impromptu dinner party in the woods, with the decorations ingeniously inspired on the spot—which in truth is not far from the mark. Finding the beautiful in nature, be it from the garden or forest or country fields, is a specialty of host Ryan Gainey's. And this special occasion tablesetting is Ryan Gainey at his best.

The dinner was to benefit the Atlanta Opera, an evening's tribute to talent on many levels—the host's for entertaining and design, the opera patrons whose success permits largesse and support, and most importantly, the talented Atlanta Opera itself. A relatively young company, the Atlanta Opera has lived up to its glorified promise—and in the very long shadow of this city's storied opera heritage.

While opera had been staged here over the years, it became an important and prestigious part of the Atlanta cultural scene in the early twentieth century. The touring company of the Metropolitan Opera first came in 1901 and again in 1905. But in 1910, Atlanta inaugurated an official opera season, whereby for one fabulous, whirlwind week, the Met was here and the city's social set revolved frenetically around luncheons, galas, dinners, dances, special events and positively sumptuous performances. It was the first time Enrico Caruso ever sang in the South, joined by famed American soprano Geraldine Farrar, and followed in time by Toscanini, Nilsson, Sills, Pavarotti, Domingo and others. It was an extraordinary thing for a small Southern city to pull off. Even the optimists were doubtful they could support it again. But Atlantans, it seems, love nothing if not a challenge, and that first year the Atlanta attendance and box office receipts were the biggest the Met had ever had. It was a time of white ties and tiaras, of ogling public throngs, and of lavish private parties during which the stars might sing out until the sun came up. Some

Atlantans still remember when, as children, they awakened to arias lilting in from the living room.

The mega-star-studded Met extravaganza continued for the next seven decades, interrupted only by the first World War and the Depression years. Then in 1987, when the go-go eighties were going-gone, the Met made its last stand in Atlanta. Its too-costly touring days were over.

In addition to the fortuitous meeting of time and circumstances, two things led to the formation of the Atlanta Opera as it is today, says its executive director, Alfred D. Kennedy Jr.: "The demise of the Met [tours] and the arrival of William Fred Scott." Former associate conductor at the Opera Company of Boston, Scott in 1985 joined what was then called the Atlanta Civic Opera as artistic director. Since then, say the critics, fairly good has gone to better, and now to best. Kennedy acknowledges, at long last, a subsiding of the back-handed compliment: "It was *wonderful—we were astounded!*" Now, says he, "They are *expecting* us to be good." And a generations-old love affair between Atlantans and opera plays out in a perpetual encore.

Menu

Grilled Fresh Mushrooms in Olive Oil and Herbs

Chicken With Artichokes, Pancetta and Cheese

Broccoli With Garlic

Apple Pecan Crisp

SERVES 4

All of these recipes can be easily doubled or even tripled. This is a good one for a crowd or a buffet, as only the casserole need be served piping hot. It's a beautiful fall menu.

Supporters of the Atlanta Opera were treated to a special performance at table by garden designer and consummate creative spirit Ryan Gainey, who hosted a dinner at home to the delight of guests and the benefit of the opera. Drinks and hors d'oeuvres were served on the terrace, which Ryan draped in muslin and dusted in autumn leaves.

Ryan offered a baguette bread pudding sprinkled with powdered sugar and served with raspberry sauce. For our bread pudding recipe, see page 155.

Grilled Fresh Mushrooms in Olive Oil and Herbs

So simple and so good. You'll need a pastry brush to brush the oil on the mushrooms.

3/4 pound heartily flavored mushrooms, such as portabello or shiitake

1/4 cup extra virgin olive oil

3 cloves garlic, minced

2 tablespoons chopped fresh parsley (flat-leaf Italian, if available)

1/2 teaspoon dried marjoram or 1/2 teaspoon dried rosemary

Salt and freshly ground pepper

Fresh parsley (or other herbs) for garnish

Prepare grill or heat oven to broil, adjusting rack to near the top. If using oven, lightly grease a cookie sheet, or spray with nonstick spray. In a small bowl, mix together olive oil, garlic, herbs and salt and pepper to taste. Wipe mushrooms clean (don't rinse them), and remove the stems. Brush mushrooms with the oil and grill or broil for 2 to 3 minutes per side, brushing again when you turn them over. Good hot or at room temperature. Garnish individual plates with parsley or other sprigs of fresh herbs.

Chicken With Artichokes, Pancetta and Cheese

You may use regular bacon instead of pancetta, and if you do, partially cook it beforehand. Then you can drain and blot it to eliminate some of its fat. You might also substitute proscuitto or paper-thin slices of salty country ham. These will change the flavor somewhat, but the dish will still be superb.

1 package frozen artichoke hearts, (thawed), or 1 can packed in water, drained
Salt
4 boned and skinless chicken breast halves (2 complete breasts)
Freshly ground pepper

4 thin slices pancetta (Italian bacon), or 4 pieces regular bacon, cut in half
1/4 cup sweet vermouth
2 medium tomatoes, chopped
1/2 cup grated, sharp cheddar cheese (reduced fat OK)

Heat oven to 350°. Place artichokes in bottom of casserole and sprinkle with a pinch of salt. Place chicken on top and sprinkle with freshly ground pepper. Drape pancetta or bacon over chicken, and pour vermouth over all. May be prepared ahead and set aside at this point. If refrigerated, bring to room temperature before resuming. Bake 50 minutes to 1 hour, spooning off fat intermittently. Combine tomatoes and cheese and sprinkle over chicken, and bake another 5 minutes or so to melt cheese.

Broccoli With Garlic

4 cups broccoli florets

1 head of garlic, peeled

¾ cup extra virgin olive oil

¼ teaspoon red pepper flakes

Salt

Steam broccoli or cook in microwave until just tender. Trim and peel all garlic cloves. In small saucepan over low heat, add oil and slowly cook garlic until golden, about 15 minutes. Drain and reserve (now wonderful garlic-flavored) oil for another use. Toss garlic with broccoli and red pepper flakes. Salt to taste. If you like you may add a tablespoon or two more of the oil, but I'd just as soon omit those calories. (1 tablespoon olive oil = 100 calories!)

Apple Pecan Crisp

There is no great art or mystery to working with phyllo pastry, you just need to pay attention. While you're working with it, keep the pastry from drying out by covering with a slightly damp tea towel. This is a pretty dessert and looks like it was a lot more trouble than it actually is. You'll need 4 custard cups or ramekins for this.

1½ pounds red or golden
   delicious apples

2 tablespoon butter

½ cup dark brown sugar,
   firmly packed

1 tablespoon cinnamon

1 tablespoon vanilla

1 tablespoon honey

1 tablespoon grated lemon zest

3 tablespoons lemon juice

⅓ cup pecan pieces

1 stick of butter, melted, or
   nonstick spray (saves on fat grams)

12 sheets phyllo dough

Powdered sugar

Core, but do not peel, apples, and cut into pieces ½ to ¾ inch in size. Melt 2 tablespoons butter in skillet and mix in brown sugar and cinnamon. Add apples and cook about 5 minutes; they should begin to soften. Add vanilla, lemon juice and zest, and honey, and cook another 3 to 5 minutes, until apples are soft but not mushy. Stir in pecans, remove from heat, and set aside.

Butter or nonstick spray each ramekin. Then, working with 1 sheet of phyllo dough at a time, spread on counter and brush with butter or spray with nonstick spray. Layer 2 more sheets over it, brushing or spraying between each one. Now, estimate (or measure, if you insist) where to cut the rectangle of pastry to make a square, with a rectangle piece left over. Lift the square and place inside the ramekin, gently pressing the pastry to fit the inside. The edges drape over the sides. Spoon 5 or 6 tablespoons of the apples into the pastry, and draw the edges up and in the middle. Take leftover rectangle of pastry and gently crumple on the top—it will look like a crumpled piece of paper. Repeat for each of the ramekins. Bake at 325° for 10 to 15 minutes, until lightly browned. To serve, remove from ramekin and place in the middle of a large dinner plate and sift a little powdered sugar over all.

A Plantation Thanksgiving

*T*n the South, quail hunting is as endemic to the cultural mystique as eating grits and saying "y'all." For good ol' boys and Southern gentlemen (and ladies) alike, what was once a means of sustenance has become not only sport but rite of passage, and, for some, a social ritual. The finely orchestrated workings of well-trained dogs and their handlers, finding the covey but not flushing it until just the right instant, the crack of a good shot—it is a beautiful thing to watch and a thrilling thing to do. And done it is, in the fall and winter, from the lowliest farms to the grandest plantations, where, truly, the quail hunt is an art form.

In the early part of this century, plantations in south Georgia and north Florida were the winter retreats of wealthy northerners. From south of Atlanta, to Thomasville, to Tallahassee, some of these plantations are still owned by the same families today, while some, no doubt, have disappeared like the way of life they once represented. Still others have adapted to the times, like *Starrsville* Plantation in Covington, about an hour's drive from Atlanta. *Starrsville* is privately owned by two families and operated as a commercial venture. Part conference center and part corporate group getaway, *Starrsville* is professionally managed and offers not only bird-shooting but sporting clays, fishing, canoeing, hiking, horseshoes, bocci and other countrified pursuits of the landed gentry.

And, as with all Southern gatherings of associates, friends and family for the purpose of having a good time, meals are to be momentous. All that fresh, country air and exercise have a way of stimulating the appetite. With fields and trees surrounding, a beautiful table awaits setting with whatever might be gathered from a walk in the woods or a roadside foray to clip colorful foliage and a few branches of berries. A stroll down the supermarket aisles yields the rest: pumpkins, cabbages and squash—who needs flowers?

Bettie Bearden Pardee is a former Atlantan and now-New Englander who, with her husband Jonathan and friends Kathy and Pete Hendricks are the owners of *Starrsville*. She is also the author of two books about entertaining and a contributing editor for *Bon Appétit* magazine. Her menu here is a new take on traditional Southern favorites and could easily carry the day for Thanksgiving, or any autumn feast to warm the heart and satisfy the soul.

*M*ENU

Field Greens With Gorganzola and Toasted Walnuts

Roasted Quail With Mushroom Stuffing

Braised Endive

Wild Rice With Pecans

Sautéed Squash

**Starrsville Sticky Toffee Pudding
With Brandied Crème Anglaise**

SERVES 8

The salad is a sublime combination of flavors. The quail are not difficult and Cornish game hens will substitute. If you think you need more than one quail per person, then adjust accordingly. The other dishes are so savory and so easy, with one word of caution, or rather, confession: Believe me, no one is more appalled than I by a recipe calling for a can of mushroom soup. There, I said it. Hell, I did it. This wild rice is so easy and so good I just can't be a snob about it. It's my own recipe—adapted long ago, probably from some Junior League cookbook back when such tomes were positively frought with cans of mushroom soup. I hope you can overlook it and just enjoy—which could apply to a lot of things in life, yes? This dessert is Bettie's original—different and good. If you are pressed for time or tradition, a pecan or pumpkin pie would go well, as would a cheesecake with a praline sauce.

Field Greens With Gorganzola and Toasted Walnuts

6 cups mixed field greens—
  Romaine, red leaf, Boston,
  arugula, raddichio, whatever

1 cup chopped walnuts, lightly toasted
1 cup crumbled Gorganzola cheese
  (blue cheese OK to substitute)

Arrange greens in bowl or individual plates. Toss with dressing (below) and sprinkle with toasted walnuts and cheese.

Red Wine Shallot Vinaigrette

1/4 cup red wine vinegar
1/2 tablespoon Dijon mustard
1 tablespoon minced shallots (optional)

1/2 teaspoon salt
1/4 teaspoon freshly ground pepper
1/2 cup olive oil

Combine all but oil. Whisking vigorously, add oil in small, steady stream. Or put it all in a tightly-lidded jar and shake.

Roasted Quail With Mushroom Stuffing

If you don't have wild quail, you can sometimes find farm-raised quail in the frozen foods section of the grocery, or your grocer could order it for you. If you don't want to bother, substitute small Cornish game hens.

8 quail, or 4 Cornish game hens
1 leek, white part only, finely chopped
  (or equivalent chopped red onion)
1/2 pound mixed wild mushrooms,
  chopped (oyster, shiitake, etc.),
  plus extra for garnish
6 slices of bacon, 2 of the slices
  diced and remaining 4 cut in half

1 tablespoon each chopped fresh
  rosemary and sage,
  plus extra for garnish
1-2 tablespoons olive oil
1/2 cup breadcrumbs
4 tablespoons (1/2 stick) butter
Toothpicks and string
  for trussing birds

Wash birds and pat dry. Rub inside and out with salt and pepper. Set aside. In a heavy pan, brown the diced bacon and remove it to drain. Wipe pan lightly, add olive oil and sauté leeks until wilted. Stir in mushrooms, rosemary, sage and diced bacon and cook for about 5 minutes. Remove from heat, stir in breadcrumbs, and salt and pepper.

Heat oven to 325°. On stove, in another heavy pan, melt butter over medium-high heat and quickly brown the birds on all sides. You may need to do this in batches. Stuff birds with mushroom mixture. Close cavity with toothpick and tie legs together with string.

Rub outsides with a little olive oil and rosemary, and lay half-slice bacon over each (2 half-slices for game hens). Roast in baking dish 20-25 minutes, basting 2 or 3 times. (Game hens will take nearly twice as long; roast until juices run clear when bird is cut with a knife.)

To serve, remove picks and string and place on platter surrounded with fresh mushrooms and sprigs of fresh rosemary and sage.

Braised Endive

8 small heads endive, trimmed
  and cut in half lengthwise
1 tablespoon fresh parsley or chervil,
  or 1 teaspoon dried

4 tablespoons (½ stick) butter
1 cup chicken stock

Sauté endive and herbs in butter for about 3 minutes, turning to coat all sides. Add stock, cover, and simmer 5 minutes. Salt to taste.

Wild Rice With Pecans

Regular brown or white rice will work for this, too, if you cannot find the wild. You may prepare it ahead and refrigerate until ready to bake.

1 cup uncooked wild rice
   (or 1 cup brown or white),
   not the fast-cooking kind
1 onion, finely chopped
1 cup pecans, coarsley
   chopped and lightly toasted

2 tablespoons melted butter
1 can cream of mushroom soup
   (reduced fat OK)
1 can beef consommé
1 can water

Heat oven to 350°. Combine all ingredients and bake, covered, for about an hour, or until the rice is done. Taste to test.

Sautéed Squash

If you cannot find baby squash (farmer's markets usually have them in season), substitute another, peeled, if necessary, and cut into bite-size pieces.

2 pounds small baby squash
1/4 cup (1/2 stick) butter

Salt

Melt butter in heavy skillet over medium-low heat. Add squash and cook for about 5 minutes. Lower heat and cover, steaming for another 4 or 5 minutes until crisp-tender. Salt to taste.

Starrsville Sticky Toffee Pudding

Fantastic and different.

8 ounces chopped dates
1 cup boiling water
2 sticks butter, softened
1 cup sugar
2 eggs, room temperature

1 teaspoon vanilla
1 1/2 cup flour
1 teaspoon baking powder
1 teaspoon baking soda

A beautiful buffet prepared by Bettie Bearden Pardee to warm the heart and satisfy the soul.

Grease a 9-inch pie plate or an 8-inch baking pan. Heat oven to 350°. Place dates in bowl and cover with boiling water. Cream butter and sugar and beat in eggs one at a time. Add vanilla. Sift flour, baking powder and baking soda into butter mixture. Fold in dates and soaking liquid. Pour into pan and bake 45 minutes to 1 hour, until springy to touch. Cut into wedges or squares and serve with the Crème Anglaise.

Brandied Crème Anglaise

4 egg yolks	$^1/_2$ cup heavy cream
$^1/_4$ cup brown sugar	2 tablespoons apple brandy
Dash salt	(or other liqueur, such as Frangelico)
1 $^1/_2$ cups milk	2 teaspooons vanilla

In saucepan, mix egg yolks, sugar and salt. Over low heat, gradually add milk and cream, stirring constantly until thickened. Do not let it boil. Remove from heat and stir in brandy or liqueur and vanilla, and pour into serving bowl, covered, to chill.

Happy Birthday!

*A*bove all, Brian Carter wants to be clear about one thing: "Birthdays are really important. If you've made it one more year, that's something to celebrate! It's a milestone and not to be taken lightly." Well! With that almost-admonition fresh in mind, Carter approaches his birthday parties with a gleeful vengeance, much to the delight of guests and friend Anita Crosby, honoree of this particular fête. A young designer and decorative painter, Carter embodies Atlanta's abundant creative spirit in the best way. His work is about originality and color, evident even in the way he entertains at home. He also is about being young, on a budget, and working with limited resources.

"I don't really have a dining room," he explains, "so I have to create one by treating it in a theatrical sense." He defines a space using wonderful painted screens and plays off a large, nearly wall-sized mirror propped on the floor. The tablecloth, napkins and matching paper hats he painted himself, all to shore up what he calls "this classic idea of a birthday party." The hats and decorations—even the old-fashioned birthday cake ablaze with candles—are slightly hokey, he admits, "But these are the birthday parties we grew up with, and they disappear once we're adult." As Carter sees it, for no good reason. "Everyone's become so *tasteful*," he decries, in his best native Savannah drawl and sarcasm.

Not that Carter's birthday *meal* was not as full of taste as it could be. Prepared at the hand of Jenny Johnston, fellow creative spirit, paralegal, and caterer-on-the-side, the evening's vegetarian fare was as satisfying as it was pretty, and easily do-able in advance. I've added a couple of appetizers just for fun. The fabulous cake is courtesy of Angie Bennett Mosier, whose arrival on the Atlanta cake scene has since inspired many an "ooh" and "ah" for her beautiful and utterly unique creations. Her cakes are arguably too pretty to taste good, and yet they are defiantly, absolutely delicious. Birthday or no, this is a menu made for "many happy returns."

Menu

Chile Cheese Layers

Baby Burger Bites

Fresh Tomato and Basil Tart

Black Bean Salad

Spinach Artichoke Casserole

Can't-Stop-Eating-It Cornbread

**Hot Milk Cake With Caramel Icing or Old Fashioned
Butter Cake With White Chocolate Buttercream Icing**

SERVES 6

With the exception of the Baby Burger Bites, which are optional, this is a vegetarian menu and perfect for easy entertaining because it can all be made in advance and nothing needs babysitting. If you'd like to add a meat or fish main course, this menu is versatile enough to accommodate beautifully a range of flavors. Quick and easy answers would be carry-out fried or roast chicken, baked ham or good, salty country ham, sliced paper thin. Grilled fish or shrimp would work well also. If you do add a meat, eliminate something else—most likely the bean dish, since you're supplying alternative protein. I also offer an alternative cake recipe and confess I am revealing one of my mama's most prized recipes—which turns out to be one of her friend's mama's most prized recipes, sworn to secrecy—until now, that is.

Chili Cheese Layers

This yummy, casual hors d'oeuvre comes from Sadie Brooks.

6 small (4-ounce) cans of green chilis, rinsed and drained

1 pound cheddar cheese, grated

1 pound Monterey Jack cheese, grated

1 8-ounce carton egg substitute, thawed (or 4 whole eggs)

4 tablespoons flour

1 small (5-ounce) can evaporated milk

1 (12-ounce) jar prepared tomato salsa, if desired

Heat oven to 350°. In a greased 9 x 13-inch baking dish, layer half the cheese, then half the chilis, then repeat. Combine egg substitute, flour and milk, and pour over. Bake 45 minutes. Cut into squares and pour salsa over top or serve on the side, if desired.

Baby Burger Bites

Kathy Servick, of the Atlanta catering company Rich Bits, is known for her delectable and unique, well, rich bits. Here is one of her most popular—and it's what everyone always talks about the next day. Kathy makes them ahead and freezes them by the dozen. Recipe is easily doubled or tripled.

1 pound ground beef

1 tablespoon minced onion

1 teaspoon salt

1/8 teaspoon pepper

Dash garlic powder

White bread

Prepared (store bought) chili sauce

Combine all ingredients except bread and chili sauce, and shape into small patties about ¾ of an inch thick and slightly less than 1 inch in diameter. (One pound of ground beef will yield 16 to 20 small patties.) Using a 1½-inch cookie cutter, cut rounds from bread and toast lightly. Press burger into toast and remove it, leaving a small indentation. Spoon a little chili sauce on the bread, then replace the burger (to be served open-faced). Wrap in plastic wrap and freeze until ready to serve. To serve, place frozen on cookie sheet and bake at 400° for 10 minutes, or until done.

Birthdays are a big deal to designer and decorative painter Brian Carter, and he sets the stage accordingly. Caterer Jenny Johnston prepared a hearty vegetarian meal as tasty as it is visually appealing

Fresh Tomato and Basil Tart

Everyone loves this.

Prepared pastry dough to make
   1 (10-inch) tart shell
8 ounces mozzarella cheese, shredded
2 tablespoons chopped, fresh basil,
   plus extra whole leaves for garnish

4-5 small ripe tomatoes (or equivalent
   plum tomatoes), cut in $\frac{1}{2}$-inch slices
   and drained on paper towels
$\frac{1}{2}$ teaspoon each salt and pepper
$\frac{1}{4}$ cup extra virgin olive oil

Preheat oven to 400°. Line 10-inch removable-bottom tart pan with pastry dough. Spread bottom of tart with cheese and sprinkle with chopped basil. Cover with tomato slices, arranging to cover as evenly as possible. Sprinkle with salt and pepper and drizzle with olive oil. Bake 30 to 40 minutes. Garnish with fresh basil and serve in wedges.

Black Bean Salad

2 cans (15 ounces each) black beans,
    rinsed and drained
2 medium tomatoes, finely chopped
1 serrano chili (jalapeño OK, too),
    seeded and finely chopped
1 cup chopped red bell pepper

$\frac{1}{2}$ cup chopped purple onion
$\frac{1}{4}$ cup white wine vinegar
2 tablespoons vegetable oil
    (olive, canola, etc.)
$\frac{1}{2}$ teaspoon salt

Mix all ingredients, cover and refrigerate at least an hour. The longer it sits, the more the flavors meld together. Makes 5 cups.

Spinach Artichoke Casserole

This is a bit of an old stand-by, but so good with so many things. Jenny has done it with nonfat cream cheese and vows it is still excellent. Save your calories for dessert.

2 (10-ounce) packages frozen,
    chopped spinach, thawed and
    squeezed as dry as possible
8 ounces cream cheese,
    softened (low fat or nonfat are OK)
1 stick butter or margarine, softened
1(14-ounce) can artichoke hearts,
    halved or quartered

1 (8-ounce) can water chestnuts,
    sliced
$\frac{1}{4}$ cup Parmesan cheese,
    plus 2 or 3 tablespoons to
    sprinkle on top
Worcestershire and Tabasco®
    sauces to season
Salt

Heat oven to 350°. Combine cream cheese and butter. Add spinach, artichoke hearts, water chestnuts and Parmesan cheese. Season to taste with Worcestershire, Tabasco® and salt. Bake for about 15 minutes, until heated through and bubbly.

Can't-Stop-Eating-It Cornbread

So-called because a friend of mine made this once for a dinner party and ate every bit of it before her company came. So easy it's almost too good to be true, but eating is believing—with just a trace of fat, to boot.

¾ cup yellow cornmeal (not self-rising)	½ teaspoon salt
1 tablespoon canola oil	1½ cups boiling water

Heat oven to 450° and grease a cookie sheet or spray with nonstick spray. Combine first 3 ingredients and stir in boiling water. It will be the consistency of thick pancake batter. Pour on cookie sheet by scant tablespoonfuls, and cook 30 to 40 minutes. You may also add chopped jalapeño chiles and/or grated cheese.

Hot Milk Cake With Caramel Icing

This cake is one of my favorite things in life. It is a real old-timey cake, and the boiled icing is the good kind that gets hard on the outside but stays moist and mushy inside. The recipe comes from the late Lillian Robinson, mother of family friend "Boo" Beasley. Mama used to make it for our birthdays and would double the icing, so it was about an inch thick in the middle—now that's love.

Hot Milk Cake

You could also use this recipe to make cupcakes.

4 eggs	2 cups self-rising flour, sifted
2 cups sugar	½ cup (1 stick) butter
1 teaspoon vanilla	1 cup milk

Heat oven to 350°. Grease 1 tube pan or 2 round layers and dust with plain, fine breadcrumbs or flour. In saucepan over low heat, or slowly in microwave, melt the butter in the milk. It should be lukewarm. Set aside. Combine eggs, sugar and va-

nilla and beat until light. Add flour slowly, then add milk mixture. Pour into pre-pared tins or pan. Bake cupcakes 30 to 35 minutes, or until tester comes out clean. Bake layers 35 to 40 minuters, regular tube cake 50 minutes.

Caramel Icing

You need a heavy saucepan and a candy thermometer. Make sure you cook the icing long enough, or it will not thicken properly. If you cook it too much, you can thin with a little more evaporated milk.

½ cup (1 stick) butter, softened
1 pound light brown sugar
½ teaspoon salt

1 small can (5 ounces) evaporated milk
½ teaspoon baking powder

Beat butter and sugar together until creamy. Add salt and milk. Boil gently, stirring constantly, until mixture reaches "soft ball" on candy thermometer, about 240°. Let sit for 5 minutes, then add baking powder. Allow to cool 10-15 minutes more, then beat until icing starts to lose its sheen and becomes spreading consistency. The beating takes a while, from 5 to 15 minutes, depending on how long the icing was cooked and how much it was allowed to cool afterwards. Ice the cake and decorate with shiny green leaves from the garden, or candied violets if you like.

Old Fashioned Butter Cake With White Chocolate Buttercream Icing

Angie is gracious enough to share her recipe. The cake pictured is this very recipe, with the addition of fondant icing on top, for the smooth surface effect. If you want to make the fondant, find a recipe in a specialty cookbook. The painting is done with food coloring and a brush.

Old Fashioned Butter Cake

6 large egg yolks,
   at room temperature
1 cup milk, room temperature
2 1/4 teaspoons vanilla
1 1/2 cups sugar
3 cups cake flour

1 tablespoon plus
   1 teaspoon baking powder
3/4 teaspoon salt
3/4 cup (1 1/2 sticks) butter,
   softened (do not substitute margarine)

Heat oven to 350°. Grease and flour two 8- or 9-inch round cake pans. Combine egg yolks, 1/4 cup of the milk and vanilla, and set aside. In bowl for electric mixer, sift together dry ingredients. Add butter and remaining milk. Mix on low speed until moist and increase speed to medium (high for hand-held mixers) for about 90 seconds. Scrape down sides and begin adding egg mixture about 1/4 cup at a time, beating for 15 to 20 seconds after each addition. Pour batter into prepared pans and bake 30 minutes or until cake tester comes out clean. While it is cooling, make the icing.

White Chocolate Buttercream Icing

Note this has no added sugar. The chocolate does the trick, but it isn't an overly sweet icing.

8 ounces cream cheese, softened

1 cup (2 sticks) butter, softened

6 ounces best quality white chocolate
(Angie uses Lindt Swiss White)

2 tablespoons fresh lemon juice

Break chocolate into little pieces and melt in double boiler over low heat, stirring constantly. Or melt in microwave, heating for 25-second intervals, stirring between each interval, until just the smallest bits are left whole. Let the residual heat finish the job as you stir. Be careful; chocolate burns easily and there's no saving it. As it cools, continue stirring to keep it creamy.

    Beat cream cheese and add lemon juice. Mixing at low speed, slowly add chocolate. Add butter and turn speed up to medium until mixed well. Use immediately or refrigerate for several days. Allow to come to room temperature before using, however.

TO ASSEMBLE

Cake

Icing

Fresh raspberries or sliced,
fresh strawberries, if desired

Let cake cool completely. Frost one layer and place berries on top. Berries should almost be touching each other. Put second layer on top and complete frosting.

Sweethearts' Dinner

*S*haron Abroms has one of the best, but not so well-kept, secrets in Atlanta: her garden. It is a storybook garden—a fairytale in flowers and plants. Heavily scented old roses and blooming vines drape over fences and trail along arbors and gates. Keeping them company are cherished "pass-along" plants from family and friends, and old favorites with old-fashioned, nostalgic names, like Love in a Puff, Hearts a Bustin', Bachelor's Buttons, and Sweet Breath of Spring. There is even an enchanting, tucked-away allée of Annabelle hydrangeas as willowy and lithe as young maidens. "It fulfills all her artistic flirtations," says Ryan Gainey, who advises Sharon in the continual planning of a botanical courtship to which she is completely devoted. For Sharon's is a garden that embraces romance as much as romance embraces a single rose.

In her house the ambiance continues—a perfect setting for Valentine's Day dinner—for sweethearts, family or a gathering of friends. A romantically inspired Ryan helped to fix things up for this intimate evening at table, choosing to avoid the clichés yet cling ever so delicately to sentiment. For a centerpiece, no red longstems but a nursery flat of forget-me-nots—innocent and unpretentious. The prettiest linens were tied with wide organza ribbons, and sprinkled overall were Sharon's own white rose petals. A statue of cupid stood vigil. The candles shone, the silver glinted and the evening sparkled.

Who was it who said food is love? And unfussy food when your love is around— is true love. Or it's a high form of thoughtfulness, at least. This menu is entirely do-ahead-able. It may even be sexy. Are there more seductive smells on earth than mussels steaming in wine and garlic, or steaks sizzling on a grill? And for the ambitious baker, the recipe for cake artist-extraordinaire Angie Mosier's cake is included. There is also a lovely (speaking of old-fashioned) dessert as an alternate: my mother's Charlotte Russe With Strawberry Sauce. Add a heart-shaped chocolate shortbread cookie or other sweet, edible valentine. And a box of chocolates goes with everything!

Menu

Mussels in White Wine, Shallots, Garlic and Parsley

Grilled Marinated Steak With Mustard Caper Sauce

New Potatoes With Wild Mushrooms and Arugula

Charlotte Russe With Strawberry Sauce
or
Angie Mosier's Heart-Shaped Cake

SERVES 6 TO 8

Mussels in White Wine, Shallots, Garlic and Parsley

When it occurred to me that mussels were the perfect starter for this menu, I called Brasserie Le Coze at Lenox Square, because theirs are the best I have ever had, anywhere. I have actually dreamt about this sauce. Chef Robert Holley kindly obliged, and this is his recipe adapted somewhat for the home cook.

Now, you (like me) may be one of those people who never wanted to mess with mussels at home because they were kind of a pain. OK, a big pain. But messing with mussels doesn't mean what it used to. Now you can get them in pretty good shape, in nice little mesh bags. All you have to do is rinse them off and trim away the "beard," or the black, thread-like thing between the shells. Look for smooth, uncracked shells and prominent beards (unless they've been cleaned already).

This is not a do-ahead dish, but it's fun to have your guests gather around in the kitchen while you do the few minutes worth of cooking they require. Then eat them in the kitchen with good bread to soak up the juices, or take them to the table. Just don't eat so many that you dull your appetite.

A pound of mussels makes a very light appetizer for 6 to 8, as the menu specifies. Do half again the recipe, or double it, if you want more.

1 pound mussels

1 tablespoon finely chopped shallots

2 tablespoons butter

½ teaspoon minced fresh garlic

½ teaspoon plus 1 tablespoon minced fresh parsley

2 tablespoons cream

¼ cup white wine

Rinse and scrub beards from mussels. In large skillet over medium heat, sauté shallots in butter, garlic and ½ teaspoon of parsley. Add cream and white wine, then mussels. Cover and cook gently until shells open, about 5 minutes. If any are still closed, remove the opened ones and cook the others a few minutes longer. Discard any that remain closed.

Serve from the skillet or ladle into individual bowls. Have good, crusty French bread on hand for dipping, and an extra plate or two for the shells.

Grilled Marinated Steak

This recipe comes from my cousin, Rena Harris, and is the best of its kind I have ever tasted. It does, however, call for a few ingredients now out of fashion for health reasons. Harrumph. There is a meat tenderizer without MSG, and an "Accent" without it, too. Use these if you like, or omit and add other seasonings as you wish.

3 to 4-pound top round steak or London broil

4 teaspoons meat tenderizer

2 tablespoons sugar

4 tablespoons sherry

4 tablespoons soy sauce

2 tablespoons honey

2 teaspoons salt

2 teaspoons Accent

Combine all ingredients and marinate beef for 6 hours or overnight, turning occasionally. Charcoal to desired doneness—10 to 12 minutes per pound for medium rare. This is very good served cold and thinly sliced. Mustard Caper Sauce is optional.

Mustard Caper Sauce

3 tablespoons grainy Dijon mustard

1 egg

1 green onion, white and
   2 inches green part chopped

1/2 teaspoon fresh marjoram,
   or 1/4 teaspoon of dried

2 tablespoons lemon juice,
   or more to taste

3/4 cup olive oil

1/4 cup cream, lightly whipped

2 tablespoons capers, drained

In processor or blender, combine mustard, egg, onion, marjoram and lemon juice. Then with machine running, add oil in a thin, steady stream. Transfer to separate bowl and fold in whipped cream and capers. If doing ahead, wait on adding cream and capers until ready to use.

New Potatoes With Wild Mushrooms and Arugula

This is fabulous. I have even served it as a meal in itself. Choose the smallest new potatoes you can find. If they are too big to be bite-sized, however, cut them in halves or quarters.

3 pounds new potatoes

1 small head of garlic,
   cloves separated but not peeled

Coarse salt

1/2 cup plus 1 tablespoon olive oil

1/2 pound wild mushrooms
   (shiitake, wood's ear, chantarelle, etc.
   or sliced portabello mushrooms,
   or combination. Dried porcini
   are also good in this.*)

1 tablespoon balsamic vinegar

2 teaspoons grainy Dijon mustard

1/2 cup (packed) arugula leaves
   or mixed field greens

4 ounces goat cheese

Freshly ground pepper

Heat oven to 300°. In roasting pan, toss potatoes and garlic with 2 tablespoons of the olive oil and sprinkle with salt. Bake 1 to 1 1/2 hours, until tender. Reduce heat if they are cooking too fast, and stir them occasionally to prevent sticking.

While the potatoes cook, sauté mushrooms for 2 or 3 minutes in 1 tablespoon olive oil, just until they release their aroma and begin to soften. Set aside.

Whisk together the mustard and vinegar and, still whisking, add remaining olive oil in a thin stream, so the dressing will emulsify and thicken. Remove potatoes from oven and remove garlic. (Put the garlic in a small bowl and bring it to the table, if you like. It is wonderful squeezed onto bread or toast.) Toss potatoes and mushrooms together with dressing. Before serving add arugula and crumble goat cheese on top. Season with freshly ground pepper. You will have none of this left over.

*You only need 4 ounces of dried porcini for this. Pour a cup of boiling water over them and soak 15 minutes before draining, chopping and adding to salad.

Charlotte Russe With Strawberry Sauce

Must be made at least 6 hours ahead.

Charlotte Russe

½ tablespoon plain gelatin

½ cup milk, divided into 1/4 cups

1 package lady fingers

2 cups whipping cream

½ cup sugar

1 teaspoon vanilla

1 tablespoon sherry, or more to taste

5 egg whites

1 pint fresh (washed) strawberries,
    if in season

Stir gelatin into 1/4 cup cold milk. Gently warm remaining 1/4 cup milk and stir gelatin mixture into it. While it cools, whip the cream until stiff, gradually stirring in sugar, vanilla and sherry. Line a pretty glass bowl with lady fingers, and sprinkle lady fingers with more sherry, if desired (I don't). Add gelatin mixture to whipped cream and blend well. Beat egg whites until stiff but not dry, and fold into whipped cream misture. Pour into lady finger-lined bowl and chill at least 6 hours. Top with fresh strawberries, if in season.

Angie Mosier created this confectionary version of a heart-shaped candy box in which to nestle her old-fashioned butter cake with white chocolate frosting and raspberries. The romantic spirit of Sharon Abrom's "storybook garden" carries on in her entertaining at home. On page 134, garden designer Ryan Gainey assisted with a flat of Forget-me-nots for the centerpiece and temporarily relocated a small statue of Cupid to hover lovingly about.

Strawberry Sauce

Serve in separate bowl, along with the russe. Completely delicious and easy. If you use frozen strawberries with no added sugar, which you can, you may want to add a tablespoon or two of sugar to the sauce.

2 (10-ounce) packages frozen strawberries in light syrup, thawed

½ teaspoon almond extract

Combine berries and extract and process or blend to reach desired consistency. Makes 2 cups.

Angie Mosier's Heart-Shaped Cake

Heart-Shaped "Box"

2 to 3 cups tempered white chocolate
   or white chocolate candy coating
   disks (available in stores that sell
   cake decorating supplies)

Heart-shaped baking pan

Lightly grease inside and edges of heart-shaped pan. Melt chocolate in microwave at 25-second intervals, stirring between each interval, until chocolate is creamy and melted. Watch it carefully.

Begin pouring the melted chocolate into the pan, turning the pan and allowing the chocolate to coat the sides. Continue until you have a thin coating all over. It will be thin, but don't worry, you will do this several times. Refrigerate and allow the first layer to cool completely (10 minutes), then repeat. At this point, you can use a small rubber spatula to help spread the coating. (The stroke marks will not show in finished cake.) Repeat a third time, then refrigerate for at least 20 minutes.

Invert pan onto wax paper-covered surface and whittle away any rough edges with a small, sharp knife. Be gentle; you have a very fragile heart here.

To make the lid for the box, grease the bottom of the pan and melt chocolate as before. Pour melted chocolate into the bottom until about 1/4 inch thick. Let cool at least 30 minutes, then carefully invert onto wax paper.

Old Fashioned Butter Cake and White Chocolate Buttercream Icing

See recipe on page 132.

TO ASSEMBLE

1 cup fresh raspberries

Decorative white icing, if desired

Trim the butter cake to fit the pan, or bake it in the heart-shaped pan to begin with (you will still need to trim it.) Place cake on something flat that you can pick up and turn over. Place chocolate box on top of cake and carefully invert so cake falls into box. Frost top of cake with icing and cover with fresh raspberries. The top of the box should fit over it. Decorate with ribbon, fresh flowers, or, as Angie does so beautifully, with flowers made from fondant icing—but I am not that advanced.

Golden Jubilee Symphony Ball

*T*n such a monumentally historic year as 1945, it is little wonder that the formation of something as inauspicious-sounding as the "Atlanta Youth Symphony Orchestra" passed as a minor footnote in the cultural life of a city pre-occupied with anything but. President Franklin D. Roosevelt died in April of that year at the Little White House in Warm Springs, Georgia. His funeral train to Washington stopped first in Atlanta, to be greeted by Mayor William B. Hartsfield, who expressed condolences to Mrs. Roosevelt. Barely one month later, Atlanta and the Allies rejoiced at the news of Germany's surrender; and in August, Mayor Hartsfield exclaimed to the throngs overflowing Peachtree Street to "Tear the roof off!" to celebrate victory in the Pacific. So it was in the midst of this that Atlantans nevertheless went about their daily lives as best they could, and a group calling themselves the Atlanta Music Club eventually signed gifted young Chicago conductor Henry Sopkin to a one-year contract as the orchestra's conductor and music director. His one year became twenty, and his group of part-time musicians became the Atlanta Symphony Orchestra.

In 1967, Robert Shaw began his illustrious tenure at ASO, having been for eleven years previously the associate conductor of the Cleveland Orchestra and director of his then rising-star-quality chorale. Maestro Shaw's leadership elevated the orchestra to world-wide status, confirmed by fourteen Grammy awards, sold-out performances in Washington, D.C., and New York City, and a highly successful European debut tour with the ASO Chorus in 1988. In that same year, the ASO baton formally passed to the internationally known conductor Yoel Levi, while Robert Shaw continues as director emeritus and conductor laureate.

Today, Yoel Levi and the Atlanta Symphony are a jewel in the crown of Atlanta's many excellent arts organizations, having completed a second European tour in 1991 to glowing reviews. Back at home, it is estimated that more than half a million people per year attend symphony performances, venues for which vary from the Woodruff Arts Center to Chastain and Piedmont parks.

Celebrating it 50th anniversary season in 1994–95, the symphony's annual fund-raising ball was held in grand style. Chaired by Frances Graves, with co-chairmen Mary Patton and Ada Lee Correll, the formal affair was entitled, appropriately, "Golden Jubilee." Decorations were executed by Event Design Group, under the creative direction of Frannie and her committee. As is the custom, guests attend a performance in the Woodruff Arts Center concert hall and proceed to a lavish dinner-dance in the galleria—dramatically transformed under a cascading canopy of twinkling white lights. It was an evening of grace notes, trilling in the measures between a history of accomplishment and a future of promise.

 ENU

Carrot Soup With Red Pepper Purée

Crab Cakes

Lemon Tagliatelle With Peas and Prosciutto

Bittersweet Chocolate Raspberry Tart

SERVES 6

Carrot Soup With Red Pepper Purée

A version of this was served at a friend's house in Highlands, N.C., and was the hit of the evening. It is a fabulous combination of flavors and makes a lovely presentation. It is also an excellent precedent to seafood. Candy Sheehan helped to re-create the recipe, which the hostess was not at liberty to divulge. Our version, by the way, has very little fat and can be served hot, room temperature or cold.

Carrot Soup

1 ½ pounds carrots,
    scraped and coarsely chopped
1 medium onion, chopped
1 tablespoon butter
4 cups chicken broth

⅓ cup orange juice
½ teaspoon salt
Pinch cayenne or red pepper
Pinch of nutmeg
2 tablespoons chopped fresh chives

In large pot, sauté carrots and onion in butter over medium heat for 5 minutes. Add chicken broth and carrots. Raise heat to medium-high and cook for 15 to 20 minutes, or until carrots are tender. Purée in blender or food processor and return to pot. Stir in orange juice, salt, cayenne, nutmeg and chives.

Red Pepper Purée

3 red bell peppers,
    seeded and quartered

1 tablespoon butter
½ cup water

Sauté peppers in butter for 5 minutes. Add water and simmer until peppers are tender, about 10 minutes. Purée in blender or food processor.

TO SERVE

Ladle soup into bowls and place a ¼-cup dollop of the red pepper mixture in the center of each. With the point of a knife at the edge of the red pepper circle, draw out a bit of the red pepper into the carrot soup, working around the circle to form a starburst design.

Crab Cakes

Jim Landon, Atlanta attorney, Renaissance man and longtime member of the Atlanta Symphony's board of trustees, is known for his nonpareil crab cakes. Here they are.

1 pound best backfin crabmeat

$^2/_3$ cup plain breadcrumbs

$^1/_2$ cup mayonnaise

1 large minced scallion,
 white and green part
 (about 2 tablespoons)

$^1/_3$ cup minced fresh parsley

$^1/_4$ teaspoon dry mustard

$^1/_4$ teaspoon freshly ground pepper

Dash of hot pepper sauce

1 egg, lightly beaten

2 tablespoons olive oil,
 (or nonstick spray) for frying

Combine all ingredients but oil, and gently shape into 12 patties. If you have time, cover and refrigerate up to 8 hours before cooking—this allows the flavors to meld. But you may also cook them right away.

 Heat oil or spray nonstick spray in skillet over medium high heat and cook cakes 2 to 3 minutes per side, until golden brown.

Lemon Tagliatelle with Peas and Prosciutto

A delicate and delectable dish with a very light lemon sauce (no cream!), green peas, and a touch of prosciutto, which you may omit if you like. This would also be good with asparagus in addition to, or instead of, the peas. You can make sauce ahead and gently re-heat it before adding to pasta.

2 tablespoons butter

1$^1/_2$ tablespoons flour

2 cups milk (low fat or nonfat OK)

$^1/_4$ cup grated Parmesan cheese,
 plus additional for serving

2 teaspoons finely grated lemon peel

$^1/_2$ teaspoon salt, or to taste

8 ounces tagliatelle pasta
 (angel hair, linguini,
 fettucini also OK)

1 10-ounce package
 frozen green peas, thawed
 frozen green peas, thawed

4 ounces prosciutto
 (or other paper-thin slices
 of salty ham), cut into
 $^1/_3$-inch-wide strips

Have all ingredients measured and within your reach. Melt butter in a large saucepan over low heat, and sprinkle flour over. Stir with a whisk until smooth and beginning to turn golden, about 3 minutes. Continue stirring and slowly pour in milk. Turn heat to medium-high and bring to a boil. Stir constantly for 8 to 12 minutes, or until sauce thickens. Blend in lemon peel, Parmesan and salt, and remove from heat.

Bring large pot of salted water to boil and cook pasta according to package directions. Drain (but do not rinse) and add to sauce. Mix in peas and prosciutto and serve. Sprinkle with additional Parmesan, if desired.

Bittersweet Chocolate Raspberry Tart

The perfect not-too-sweet but so satisfying finish to a rich meal. This, too, was inspired by Jim Landon, who divines a similarity using Nutella brand chocolate as the layer for the fresh berries. If you can find Nutella, by all means try it, though it is sweeter than the bittersweet chocolate. Just about any fruit or nut-flavored liqueur could be substituted for the Frangelico. You may also use this recipe to make individual tarts.

1 pastry crust for 9- or 10-inch tart	1 teaspoon vanilla
4 tablespoons (½ stick) butter, softened	2 teaspoons hazelnut liqueur,
3 tablespoons sugar	such as Frangelico
4 ounces unsweetened chocolate	(or substitute, optional)
2 tablespoons honey	2 cups fresh raspberries,
2 tablespoons cream (milk OK)	rinsed and dried

Place pastry in 9- or 10-inch tart pan with removable bottom and bake at 450° for 10 to 12 minutes, or according to your recipe or package instructions. Cream butter and sugar until light and fluffy. Melt chocolate in double boiler or microwave and add to butter mixture. Stir in cream, honey, vanilla and liqueur, if using. Spread in bottom of tart and top with fresh raspberries. Chill until serving.

Celebrating the Winter Solstice

*T*t is the shortest day and the longest night, and yet the winter solstice was celebrated in ancient cultures as a time of awakening. Though it marks the beginning of winter, says noted Atlanta horticulturist, plantsman and designer Ryan Gainey, it is also the beginning of the earth's re-birth. "It is something we may not be cognizant of, but something is definitely happening—we are beginning to move into spring." And though Atlanta is Southern and therefore usually spared a harsh winter, the city's change from bare branches of winter to luminous blossoms of spring is beautiful and dramatic.

As one especially attuned to the rhythms of nature and the cycle of seasons, Gainey habitually thinks in terms of the garden—whether designing the extravagant charity galas for which he has become famous, or on a smaller scale, entertaining friends at home. For this intimate celebration of solstice, it means gathering what is evergreen or fresh and drawing upon what has been stored for the winter. The table is decorated simply with ivy and greens, and sumptuously with silver bearing ivy and greenery motifs, courtesy Beverly Bremer Silver Shop. "It all has meaning," Gainey explains. "In mythology, ivy is considered a male symbol. And in mythological terms, the winter solstice is when the masculine side of nature begins to diminish, and the feminine side starts to grow, signaling new life."

For food, pantry items such as dried beans, herbs and fruits, and home-canned goods might be served in combinations with winter greens such as kale, cabbage and turnips. A harbinger of spring might be lamb added to a stew, while a farewell to winter might be cranberries in the dessert—both of which we've done here. And although these days one's market choices are rarely limited to what is actually growing nearby, such observances can enrich the experience of a meal by reminding us of our part in nature, and of its seasonal gifts.

Lamb and Bean Stew With Pistou

Green Salad With Chutney and Garlic Dressing

Lemon and Cranberry Bread Pudding

SERVES 6 TO 8

I have to confess this is one of my favorites, and everything can be prepared ahead. The lamb stew is a recipe I arrived at after much experimenting, and it is one of the biggest crowd-pleasers in my repertoire. Serve it with good bread for sopping— which you can't help doing. About the dried beans: Rinsing, soaking and cooking them takes a long time. I gave it up, but if you are a purist, follow your own method or the package directions. As an hors d'oeuvre, have cheese straws, olives or nuts just for the sake of a nibble, but not much else. You just don't need it with this menu. (Besides, my mama used to say serving heavy hors d'oeuvres was a sign of in-security. She usually said this when time was running short.) Serve the stew by itself, with good, whole-grain or French bread—the stew has everything in the world in it and is an ample meal in itself. I like serving the salad after the stew; it lightens things up and clears the palate between a hearty main course and a substantial, though not heavy, dessert.

Lamb and Bean Stew With Pistou

Lamb and Bean Stew

This may be the number-one favorite all-around recipe in this book. A sure thing. Just know your guests will want seconds, and don't count on any leftovers.

Of course good things take time. This involves a lot of chopping and therefore a lot of time. You can chop and slice these vegetables into pretty little uniform pieces if you want to, but I do it all in the food processor—the onion with the chopping blade; the celery, carrot and cabbage with the slicing blade. Do all the preparation work in advance, then it goes fairly quickly, and you can be working on something else while it's simmering.

1 piece of bacon
2 pounds lean lamb,
   cut into ¾-inch chunks
Coarse salt and
   freshly ground pepper
6 cups chicken, vegetable
   or beef broth
2 celery stalks, chopped
1½ cups chopped carrots
2 cups chopped onion
1 (14-ounce) can tomatoes
2 cups chopped cabbage

1 teaspoon dried marjoram
   or rosemary or both
1 teaspoon dried basil
¾ cup dried porcini,
   soaked in 1 cup boiling water
   (If you cannot find these or
   other dried mushrooms,
   it is not the end of the world,
   but they do add a special flavor.)
2 (14-ounce) cans Great Northern
   or white kidney beans,
   rinsed and drained

In a large, non-stick pot, fry the bacon until brown but not crisp. Remove, leaving grease in the pot, and dice the bacon—you'll add it back later. In the same pot, over medium high heat, brown the lamb in batches, seasoning with salt and pepper. Set it aside, in the same bowl with the bacon, if you like.

Now, still in the same pot, add the celery, carrot and onion, cooking until soft. If you need more liquid, add a little of the chicken stock or juice from the canned tomatoes. Add the tomatoes, with their juice, breaking them up with the spoon. Stir in the herbs, then the stock, stirring and scraping bits from the bottom of the pot. Add the cabbage, lamb, porcini and their soaking liquid, cover and simmer ½ hour.

Add beans and simmer another ½ hour. Meanwhile, make the pistou.

Pistou

4-5 cloves garlic, crushed

1 teaspoon coarse salt

¾ cup Fontina, Munster
   or Gouda cheese, grated

¼ cup Parmesan cheese, grated

2 tablespoons olive oil

Mash all ingredients together, then stir in about ½ cup of the stew broth. Set aside. Just before serving, stir the pistou into the stew.

Green Salad With Chutney and Garlic Dressing

Romaine, arugula, raddichio, endive, and red leaf lettuce—or any combination thereof.

Chutney and Garlic Dressing

Atlanta chef William Witt whipped up this dressing for a dinner party and everyone raved. I called him first thing the next morning for the recipe. William uses Major Grey's chutney, by the way, and opts for mild-tasting vegetable oil such as canola or safflower, which lets the chutney and garlic flavors come through fully. William also put fresh basil leaves in the salad—wonderful.

½ cup vegetable oil

⅓ cup water

¼ cup chutney

2 tablespoons lemon juice

2 cloves garlic, chopped

½ teaspoon red pepper flakes

Salt

Combine all ingredients except oil and salt in food processor or blender. With machine running, add oil in a slow, thin stream and process until smooth. Salt to taste.

Lemon Cranberry Bread Pudding

Atlanta baker Angie Mosier helped develop this recipe, which is a departure from ordinary bread pudding and oh, sooo good. Serve warm, room temperature or cool.

Cranberry Compote

1 (16-ounce) can whole-berry
    cranberry sauce

$^{1}/_{4}$ cup orange-flavored liqueur,
    brandy or bourbon

Combine cranberries and liqueur in small saucepan and cook over low heat, stirring until mixed well and hot, but not boiling (about 3 minutes). Remove from heat and allow to thicken slightly.

Though it is the shortest day and the longest night, the winter solstice marks the beginning of winter's end and spring's awakening. At this table, chez Gainey, the use of ivy and evergreens is simple, elegant and appropriately symbolic. The citrus-y freshness of lemon bread pudding with cranberry sauce (photo on page 154) is a comforting finish. Silver is courtesy of Beverly Bremer Silver shop.

Lemon Curd

1 ½ cups water	Dash salt
1 cup sugar	Juice and grated rind of 2 large lemons
5 tablespoons cornstarch	3 egg yolks

Measure water into top of double boiler or heavy saucepan and turn heat on low. Combine sugar, cornstarch and salt until well blended. Turn heat up on water to boil, and just as it boils pour sugar mixture into it. (Don't wait, or the water will boil away, and your measurements will be off.) Turn heat back to low and stir constantly until mixture thickens. Meanwhile, combine yolks with lemon juice and rind, and stir a tablespoon or two of the hot mixture into yolks. (This is to warm it, so the yolks will not cook when you add them back to the hot sugar.) Add entire yolk mixture back to sugar mixture and cook, stirring constantly until thick and smooth—about 10 minutes. Chill.

Bread Pudding

1 loaf (8 to 12 ounces)
  French or Italian bread,
  the staler the better
10 eggs, or equivalent egg substitute

1 cup sugar
1 quart milk
2 teaspoons vanilla extract

Slice bread into ½-inch thick slices and toast until dry but not browned. If slices are already dry, i.e. stale, you can shorten this step or skip it completely. Butter a large baking dish, approximately 10 x 15 x 2 inches. Have lemon filling and cranberries nearby. In a separate bowl, beat together eggs and sugar, then stir in milk and vanilla. Set aside. In the buttered dish, make one layer of bread slices, filling in holes with smaller pieces of bread. Spread ⅓ of the cranberries over the bread, and spoon ½ the lemon mixture over that. Repeat the layers once more: bread, cranberries, lemon. Stir egg mixture again and slowly pour over bread. Let stand at room temperature for one hour. With 5 minutes or so left, preheat oven to 350°. Place pan on cookie sheet or in a large pan with sides, and fill with water halfway up the sides of the pudding pan. I usually put the pans in the oven first, then pour in the water. Bake for about 45 minutes, until puffed and slightly golden colored.

Use the remaining ⅓ of the cranberries to spoon onto dessert plates and place a square of pudding atop it. You may also spread a little of the cranberries on top and finish with a twist of lemon peel.

Recipe Index

Index